W9-AVZ-381

GRAY
MATTER

Sleep and Dreaming

GRAY MATTER

GRAY
MATTER

Sleep and Dreaming

Marvin Rosen

CHELSEA HOUSE
P U B L I S H E R S
A Haights Cross Communications Company ®
Philadelphia

CHELSEA HOUSE PUBLISHERS

VP, NEW PRODUCT DEVELOPMENT Sally Cheney
DIRECTOR OF PRODUCTION Kim Shinners
CREATIVE MANAGER Takeshi Takahashi
MANUFACTURING MANAGER Diann Grasse
PRODUCTION EDITOR Noelle Nardone
PHOTO EDITOR Sarah Bloom

STAFF FOR SLEEP AND DREAMING

DEVELOPMENTAL EDITOR Carol Field
PROJECT MANAGER Pat Mrozek
PHOTO EDITOR Robin Landry
SERIES AND COVER DESIGNER Terry Mallon
LAYOUT Maryland Composition Company, Inc.

A Haights Cross Communications ✦ Company ®

www.chelseahouse.com

First Printing

10 9 8 7 6 5 4 3 2 1

Library of Congress Cataloging-in-Publication Data

Rosen, Marvin
    Sleep and dreaming / Marvin Rosen.
    p. cm. — (Gray Matter)
Includes bibliographical references and index.
    ISBN 0-7910-8639-9
1. Sleep. 2. Dreams. I. Title II. Series.
QP425.R328 2005
621.8'21—dc22   2005011689

All links, web addresses, and Internet search terms were checked and verified to be correct at
the time of publication. Because of the dynamic nature of the web, some addresses and links
may have changed since publication and may no longer be valid.

Contents

1 A Variety of Conscious Experiences

And He said: "Hear my words. If there be a prophet among you, I, the Lord, will make myself known to him in a vision and will speak unto him in a dream."
—Numbers 12:6

There is something about sleep that fires the imagination. What is sleep? Why do we need it? Do we really need eight hours a day? What if we get less? Dreams intrigue us even more. There is no end to the books you can find to guide you in interpreting your dreams. Look in the "New Age" section of the library or your favorite bookstore. You will find guides and atlases to explain that dreams about flying mean one thing, and dreams about water another. "Unlock the secrets of your dreams . . ." one such book promises. Type the word "dream" into your Internet server and you will find hundreds if not thousands of self-styled experts who will offer to interpret your dreams—for a price. All this is despite the fact that even Sigmund Freud, the father of modern dream analysis, warned against attributing universal meanings to dream images. According to Freud, water may mean one thing to one person and something quite different to someone else. Dreams are individual. You may recently have had a dream that worried or frightened you. Do dreams

Figure 1.1 Hypnos, the Greek god of sleep, is shown in this sculpture from the 1st or 2nd century A.D. He was the twin brother of Thanatos, the god of death.

come true? Do they reveal the future? What do dreams mean? Could anything so weird have any real relevance to the real world?

The history of thinking and research about sleep and dreams traces back to the ancients. Night and dark were considered to be mysterious and were the source of fear and superstition. In many cultures, sleep was associated with death. In ancient Greece, Hypnos was the god of sleep. His name is the origin of the word *hypnotism*, which was thought to be a kind of sleep. Thanatos, the god of death, was his twin (Figure 1.1).

According to the ancient Greeks, dreams were an entity inside the body but separate from it. They were identified with the soul. Some people believed that at night, the soul left the body and wandered in the spirit world. Others believed that dreams provided sacred guidance for daily life. The Greek philosophers sought physical explanations for sleep. Some felt it was imposed upon the brain when cranial blood vessels became filled with blood during the night. Others attributed sleep to vapors that entered the brain after escaping from decomposed food. The blood vessel theory survived through the 18th century. Nineteenth-century philosophers believed that sleep was caused by a lack of stimulation, which shut the brain down. They suggested that the brain needed to be "cranked up" to operate.

Sleep research was not taken seriously until the invention of the **electroencephalograph** (**EEG**) in 1929. The EEG records electrical activity in the form of **brain waves** from various areas of the brain through electrodes attached to the scalp. The EEG provided scientific respectability to sleep research and led to the discovery of rapid eye movement (REM) sleep by Dr. Nathaniel Kleitman and his assistant Eugene Aserinsky. Dr. Kleitman, a physiologist, was the first scientist to devote his entire career to the study of sleep. He became a professor of physiology at the University of Chicago in the early 1920s and established the first sleep laboratory. Initially, Dr. Aserinsky observed that infants rapidly moved their eyes during a certain phase of sleep. These movements, which had never before been noticed, were more visible in infants because of their thin eyelids. Later, the same observation was made with adults by placing electrodes on their eyelids. When adult subjects were awakened during REM sleep and asked, "Were you dreaming just now?" it became evident that **REM sleep** was associated with dreaming. After that discovery, there was increasing interest in sleep research.

Despite a burgeoning interest in sleep and sleep-related issues, scientists today still do not know precisely what sleep is designed to accomplish. Research conducted within the past few years suggests that it is not for relaxing the body. Body parts do not need sleep. Muscles, for example, require only brief rest periods to maintain their ability to contract. Some muscles, such as those in the heart and eye, continue to contract even during sleep. Current neurological theories state that sleep is related more to maintenance of brain function than body function. New techniques of studying the brain have yielded new ways of understanding brain function. Since the 1930s—when micro-electrodes and the **oscilloscope** were developed—neuroscientists have been able to record the firing of individual nerve cells in the brain. Recently, neuroscientists have developed electrodes small enough, and computers powerful enough, to record the simul-taneous firings of 50 to 100 nerve cells. This has allowed re-searchers to study changing patterns of nerve cell firing and to observe differences between waking and sleeping states. These studies have generated surprising new theories about why we sleep.

The study of dreams began in earnest during the early part of the 20th century, when Sigmund Freud (Figure 1.2), an Aus-trian physician and neurologist, began using dream interpreta-tion to treat "hysterical" patients with physical symptoms but no identifiable physical defects. Dreams, Freud believed, could provide these patients with insight into their unconscious wishes. The end technique of his new theory, called **psychoanal-ysis**, became the rage in Europe as well as the United States. Freud's theory assumed the existence of a submerged part of the personality called the "**id**," which consisted of socially unac-ceptable aggressive, destructive, and sexual impulses and de-sires. These impulses were kept out of conscious awareness by a more rational "**ego**" and a punishing "**superego**," or conscience. In addition to the interpretation of dreams, in which these im-pulses and wishes were expressed in a disguised form, psycho-analysis used a technique of "**free association**" under relaxed conditions, to allow unconscious thoughts to surface. The indi-vidual would be asked to allow his or her mind to wander, ver-balizing his or her other thoughts and withholding nothing. The revelation that our behavior and physical symptoms had

Figure 1.2 Sigmund Freud is the father of modern psychotherapy. He used dream analysis to uncover hidden internal conflicts.

hidden roots and that uncovering these wishes could provide a cure was controversial but exciting to many people.

Today, psychologists and neuroscientists disagree among themselves about dreams. Some believe that dreams are totally without meaning, nothing more than noise in the nervous system, and are critical of those who ascribe meaning to them. Others insist that, even if dreams have some meaning, dream content is so complex that it defies any attempt to decipher it. Yet there are those who believe that anything produced by our brain must in some way reflect our needs or personality. They find ways of gleaning meaning, even while trying to adhere to objective, scientific methods of observation and drawing conclusions. The latter is the orientation underlying this book. It is our purpose here to provide some understanding of sleep and the process of dreaming, to provide some order based on objective evidence, and to place sleep and dreaming in the perspective of human conscious experience. In so doing, we will debunk some misconceptions, answer some questions, and pose others—which we will leave unanswered. We will draw upon the sciences of biology and psychology and explore how the two intersect. We will endorse a critical attitude and healthy objectivity and skepticism in the understanding of sleep and dreams, based upon what has been scientifically determined. We hope this book will allow you to wrap your mind around possibilities that, while unproven, may provide a source for new hypotheses and research. We hope this book will give you a better understanding of yourself, and help you apply new insights for personal growth.

■ **Learn more about altered states of consciousness** Search the Internet for *eidetic imagery*, *hypnogogic state*, and *lucid dreaming*.

Imagine you are sitting in your American history class. Bored with your teacher's explanation of the Magna Carta, you turn your attention to your fellow classmates. The pretty redhead in the third row is writing a note to her boyfriend. The jock sitting in front of you seems half asleep—probably thinking about his bonehead play last Saturday. Your homeroom buddy *is* actually sound asleep in the back—if he starts snoring, he is going to get in trouble. A few kids in the front row seem to be concentrating on the teacher, or at least trying to give the impression that they are. And that annoying tag on the collar of your new shirt is *really* irritating your neck. . . .

Attention is selective. It may be focused, as when you concentrate on some important task, or it may be diffuse and wandering, seemingly without direction. Problem solving requires focused attention. Some people are better at this than others. Daydreaming allows your mind to wander, to indulge in pleasant fantasies like, "Gee, wouldn't it be great to be done with school for the summer and be surfing at the beach?"

Normal waking consciousness is only part of a wide range of conscious experience. Other forms of **conscious awareness** include dreams, **hallucinations** (which may occur in certain forms of mental illness or with drug use, specific types of religious experiences, hypnosis, or meditation), and **eidetic imagery**, a vivid recall of visual images suggesting heightened awareness. There are also levels of conscious awareness of thoughts and memories characteristic of each of the above examples. Some may be central in focus and attention, whereas others may reside barely at the fringe of consciousness or beyond, yet still influence our behavior. Psychologists apply the terms *preconscious* or *unconscious* to refer to these processes. In this view, consciousness may be thought of as a continuum of experiences from being fully aware to completely unaware. Preconscious would be an intermediate stage of awareness. This is a concept of depth, implying the ease with which ideas can be accessed. Preconscious events have a greater likelihood of becoming conscious than do unconscious events. When you put on your shirt in the morning, you can feel the material touch your skin. After a few minutes, you are no longer aware of that feeling, except if you direct your attention to it once more—if the tag on your shirt is scratching you, for example. Most people can do two or more things at once, such as driving and listening to the radio. For most people, driving becomes so automatic that attention can be directed to their favorite pop star. Older people report the unsettling experience of entering a room, perhaps to make a cup of coffee, and momentarily forgetting what it was they intended to do. On a visit to Paris, the author was pleasantly surprised when his high school French seemed to return to him. He suddenly found himself remembering words and phrases he thought he had long forgotten. This learning was there but previously inaccessible. Consciousness, according to Freud, was not an all-or-nothing phenomenon. This experience suggests that there are levels of conscious awareness that may, under the right conditions, become available. Our attention to details is selective and depends upon environmental cues, motivation, and other factors. They are preconscious because, under certain and often minimal conditions, such as hearing French words spoken, they become conscious.

Unconscious events are less likely than preconscious events to surface to our awareness, but many psychologists believe that they influence behavior nevertheless. Some psychologists further believe that dreams include content that is normally unavailable to conscious awareness. Sometimes a slip of the tongue will reveal a belief or fear that is normally not something the individual wants to reveal, or even be aware of. There are a number of emotional disorders, such as **multiple personalities, fugue states**, and **amnesia**, in which a part of the personality seems to split off and remain outside normal conscious awareness. Finally, there are reports of seemingly unnatural experiences, such as those that sometimes occur to people near death or to people attending séances (see "The Séance" box). Near-death experiences have been reported by people revived from a severe trauma. These reports share a number of common features, including traveling down a dark tunnel, seeing a bright light at the end, and being greeted by deceased friends and relatives. Séances are gatherings in which a leader who claims to be able to communicate with the dead attempts to reach a specific dead person and deliver or receive a message. Many of these experiences have been explained as natural phenomena (e.g., trickery; hypnotic phenomena); others are more difficult to understand. In this book, we explore sleeping as only one of a number of stages, levels, and varieties of consciousness.

DAYDREAMS AND FANTASY

Everyone daydreams. We let our imagination wander and fantasize about what it would be like if we were superheroes, movie

The Séance

A college student was asked to write a paper dealing with a historical place. Rather than choosing Valley Forge, Independence Hall, or the Liberty Bell, all of which were nearby historical sites, she chose to research a suburban inn and restaurant that dated back to Revolutionary War times. When she learned that a séance was going to be conducted at the inn, she asked to be included and was invited to attend. During the session, she suddenly felt as if her body had been taken over. She began speaking in a strange voice, the voice of a man who identified himself as a stable groom during the late 18th century. When the "spirit" left her body, she felt him give her a shove, which knocked her from her chair, breaking the heel of her shoe in the process. The woman continues to believe that her experience was real.

stars, or rock musicians. Sexual fantasies occur with great frequency in adolescents and adults. We find ourselves daydreaming in everyday situations—in the classroom, on the job, walking down the street, driving a car. Daydreams can be productive in allowing us to imagine what could be possible. They can motivate us and help us plan ways to make new, exciting things happen. They can also be destructive if they take our minds off what we are doing in critical situations like driving. Some people fantasize more than others. The play of children with dolls or stuffed animals is a kind of daydreaming. Imaginary friends are not uncommon in early childhood. Excessive daydreaming, though, can be used as an escape and can be a sign of emotional disorder when they preoccupy the individual and substitute for reality-based thinking and behavior.

HYPNOGOGIC IMAGERY

Between wakefulness and sleep, some people experience vivid images that are almost like hallucinations. These may occur while falling asleep or just before awakening. One subject reported that the images were like a series of slides occurring in succession, and beyond her voluntary control. Another subject found himself knowing things that he did not realize he knew. Some people anticipate the sound of their alarm clock before it actually goes off. Although these occurrences (thoughts and images) are not well understood, they may account for fantastic "otherworldly" experiences.

LUCID DREAMS

Some dreams have a peculiar characteristic. The dreamer recognizes within the dream that he or she is dreaming. Such dreams are called "**lucid dreams**." Dreamers report this to be a very satisfying state. If the dream involves fear or unpleasant events, the dreamer can reassure him- or herself that it is only a dream and that he or she will soon awaken. Some dreamers report that they can will themselves to wake up from a frightening dream. Stephen La Berge of the Stanford University Sleep Center and director of the Lucidity Institute studied lucid dreams under controlled laboratory conditions. The results of his studies are reported in a 1981 article in *Psychology Today*. Subjects were wired to an EEG. La Berge was able to train people to have lucid dreams and to signal to observers at the laboratory that they were dreaming using prearranged eye movements. Skeptics of this type of dreaming suggest that the dreamer is not really asleep. Yet there is evidence that REM sleep is occurring during lucid dreams. La Berge believes that the significance of lucid dreams is that they allow the dreamer to take responsibility for both his or her dreams and waking activities. If this is true, the technique may have important applications in psychotherapy. Subjects might be instructed, for example, to dream about their most serious concerns and to find a solution in the dream. La Berge suggests that lucid dreaming is a useful strategy for helping people face their problems.

Not everyone is successful at producing lucid dreams. The author of this book, Rosen, attempted to dream of flying by rehearsing thoughts of flying like a bird before going to sleep. Flying dreams are reported to be extremely pleasant. He did dream of flying, but it was in an airplane piloted by his friend—a recent, not-so-pleasant experience.

HYPNOSIS

Hypnosis, as a stage procedure as well as a technique now used in psychotherapy, traces back to the late 18th century. Originally, hypnotism was thought to involve a harnessing of cosmic forces, similar to magnetism. Hypnosis produces behaviors that are markedly different from what is typical or normal for the individual in question. Whether or not it represents an altered state

Figure 1.3 A young man responds to the suggestions of a hypnothera-pist. Here, the therapist has suggested to the subject that he has a bal-loon tied to his left hand and that his right hand is very heavy. The sub-ject's left arm has raised and right arm lowered accordingly.

of consciousness is the subject of great controversy among those who study this phenomenon. Some scientists believe it represents **dissociation**, or splitting of consciousness, similar to what occurs in amnesia or fugue states, both of which involve a loss of memory for recent events. Others insist that hypnosis can be explained solely on the basis of suggestion or role-playing. It has been used to reduce pain in childbirth and surgery. Some therapists use hypnosis to change inappropriate or self-defeating behavior, such as smoking. It is another example of the many ways conscious awareness can manifest itself or be altered (Figure 1.3).

MEDITATION

Western psychology has two strong influences—**psychoanalytic thought**, which deals with conflicting personality structures and unconscious motivations, and **behaviorism**, which focuses

Figure 1.4 A woman meditates outdoors. The practice of meditation is becoming increasingly popular in Western society.

exclusively on observable and measurable behaviors. It has largely avoided religious influences. In recent years, however, there have been attempts to integrate Eastern philosophy and understanding into some areas of Western thought and practice. Buddhism, which originated in India, China, and Tibet thousands of years ago, has offered approaches to increasing self-awareness and personal adjustment. Meditation, which originated with Buddhism but does not require adherence to its religious philosophy, has gained considerable popularity in Western cultures (Figure 1.4).

Meditation is designed to alter one's state of attention to a high degree of focus and to allow free rein to thoughts and emotional states. It accomplishes a nondefensive awareness of the self that may at times be quite unpleasant but can also bring about great happiness and serenity. The subjective experiences that occur during meditation represent another variation of conscious awareness.

HALLUCINATIONS

Hallucinations are vivid sensory images that occur without sensory input. The hallucinating individual may see, hear, or even smell things that are not there. Hallucinations may occur in serious mental disorders called **psychoses.** In a form of psychosis called paranoia, the individual may hear voices coming from inanimate objects, such as a radiator or radio, that command him or her to do things and that confirm feelings of persecution or delusions (false beliefs) of grandeur. Victims of trauma may experience "flashbacks" of the traumatizing event that are hallucinatory in nature.

DRUG STATES

Hallucinations may also be caused by drug states after consumption of substances such as marijuana (Figure 1.5), LSD, or PCP ("angel dust"). Psychoactive drugs alter perceptions and mood. Depressants such as alcohol, barbiturates, and opiates reduce anxiety but can impair memory and judgment. Opiates such as morphine and heroin reduce pain but can become addictive and produce severe withdrawal symptoms. Stimulants such as caffeine, nicotine, and amphetamines ("speed") increase wakefulness and energy but later can cause tiredness, irritability, headaches, and depression.

Figure 1.5 A teenage girl experiments with marijuana. Marijuana and other psychoactive drugs can alter perceptions and moods.

EIDETIC IMAGERY

While most people can remember what they have seen to some degree, their memories are often vague and inaccurate as to detail. Some people, however, have an almost photographic recall of what they have seen. These people, few in number, can look briefly at a picture and, then, when it is removed, retain an image of what they have seen with great clarity. Psychologists label this type of photographic memory eidetic imagery. It is more prevalent in children than in adolescents or adults, yet only

Eidetic Imagery: Historical Background

Francis Galton (1822–1911), the first person to describe eidetic imagery, had a marked influence on the development of psychology as a field of study. Galton, a cousin, follower, and friend of Charles Darwin (who originated the theory of evolution), inherited a great deal of money at age 22. He devoted himself to biological research, becoming interested in individual differences among people. He pioneered the idea that psychological tests could be devised to measure these differences and began studying many types of people, from geniuses to criminals. He studied the process of association and developed a theory of intelligence. Influenced by his cousin, he believed that mental processes served the purpose of helping a person adjust to the world. Galton published *Hereditary Genius*, which examined the lives of very bright, productive people. He also studied twins to determine the contributions of nature and nurture to personality and behavior. He developed statistical procedures that are still used today. In 1870, Galton published a report on the eidetic imagery of 170 schoolboys and found that 10% had the ability to recall images with great accuracy. His work predated and paved the way for the development of intelligence tests, twin studies, word association tests, correlation studies, and studies of imagery.

about 5% of children have this ability. These children can provide a wealth of detail about the images, providing even irrelevant details such as the number of buttons on a jacket the person in the picture was wearing. Some people with this gift have been reported to be able to "read" from a retained image of a page of a book. It is debatable whether eidetic imagery really represents another state of conscious awareness or is merely an enhanced form of visual memory (see "Eidetic Imagery: Historical Background" box).

UNUSUAL AND "OTHERWORLDLY" EXPERIENCES

Some people report strange experiences such as communicating with the dead, being abducted by aliens and taken to distant planets, leaving their body at night to travel to faraway places, near-death experiences, encountering ghosts, or meeting angels, saints, or Jesus (see "Near-Death Experiences" box). Such claims, when investigated scientifically, usually

Near-Death Experiences

In 1976, Raymond Moody described the occurrence of near-death experiences from interviews with people who had survived such events. There is a similarity among such reports, which seems to suggest the existence of a mind or soul that leaves the body at death. The individual hears himself pronounced dead. He hears a loud noise and feels himself being drawn into a long, dark tunnel. He feels himself outside of his physical body. Friends and relatives, long dead, come to greet him. He feels a warm, loving spirit about him. He is overwhelmed with feelings of love, joy, and peace. Despite all this, he becomes somehow reunited with his body and returns to life. Are these reports to be believed as real . . . or are they the result of hallucinations created by conditions of trauma or reduced oxygen?

remain unsubstantiated. Phenomena like these tend to be grounded in faith, not science. Yet many scientists have religious beliefs. Hard sciences today such as physics and astronomy have moved toward an openness to philosophical and mathematical constructs and not solely **empirical**, objective evidence. Some astronomers have embraced the theory that the unique circumstances that allowed for the existence of life on our planet could not have been an accident and so must be attributed to some guiding force. Similarly, some physicists are excited by "**string theory**," a universal explanation of all things from subatomic particles to the structure of the universe. String theory postulates that the most elementary building blocks of matter consist, not of particles, but of minute energy bundles that resemble strings. Many scientists believe that string theory can never be proven. Can string theory provide the unifying link between mind and body? Between nerve impulses and conscious thought and dreams?

Sleep in Perspective

In the context of the variety of conscious states a person may experience, sleep and even dream imagery may seem less unique. Once it is accepted that sleep is not a matter of the brain shutting down but an active, complex brain activity, then sleep is only a part of a total range of behavior and experiences that are all somehow related and that all have neurological foundations. The experiences can be located along several unifying dimensions. The first dimension is the level of internal, voluntary control or direction that is exerted by the individual. During sleep, the brain releases conscious control of events. In insomnia, this release of control does not take place readily. Dreams also appear to be without control, except in the case of lucid dreams. During hypnosis, control is given by default to the person inducing the hypnotic state. Hypnosis may appear to be a sleep-like state, but it does not share brain wave similarities. During meditation, the individual allows his or her mind to wander in an unfocussed manner, expanding conscious awareness of thoughts and feelings that are usually not consciously addressed.

A second unifying dimension is the level of reality of the subjective experience. Hallucinations stray far from what is real. Unless you believe in the supernatural, "otherworldly" experiences cannot be accepted as real. Dreams may be bizarre unless you can decipher a real meaning. Eidetic imagery represents an unusual level of focus on the reality of a complex visual stimulus.

Morpheus

"King Sleep was father of a thousand sons—indeed a tribe—and of them all, the one he chose was Morpheus, who had such skill in miming any human form at will. No other god can match his artistry in counterfeiting man: their voice, their gait, their face—their moods; and, too, he imitates their dress precisely and the words they use most frequently. But he mimes only men. . . ."

(Ovid, *Metamorphoses*)

Metamorphoses, Ovid (43 B.C.–A.D. 18)

Morpheus was the god of dreams in Greek mythology. According to the Roman poet Ovid, he was the son of Hypnos, the god of sleep. We no longer attribute bodily functions to individual gods. Belief in such deities has been replaced by our understanding of genetics, hormones, body chemistry, neurotransmitters, and specific functions of the brain and nervous system. Morpheus and Hypnos reside not only in the mythology of Mount Olympus, but also in the sleep centers of the brain.

A third unifying dimension is the level of focus the experience demands. During hypnosis, the individual focuses exclusively on the voice of the hypnotist, who seems to assume control of the subject's behavior and experiences. Meditation, daydreaming, and fantasy involve little structure, or focus as the individual allows his or her thoughts to wander. Hypnogogical experiences may be an early phase of sleep, whereas out-of-body experiences and "otherworldly" encounters are typically explained as dreams or hallucinations.

Sleep and dreams are natural phenomena, similar to other states, but unique as well. Both are biologically and psychologically based, both rely to some degree on external stimulation or lack of it, and both represent internal mechanisms (see "Morpheus" box).

2 | The Biology of Sleep

Modern technology and the enthusiasm of scientists devoted to a better understanding of sleep and its relation to physical and mental health led to important breakthroughs in understanding sleep and dreaming. The invention of the electroencephalograph (EEG) by Hans Berger in 1929 was a watershed event. The reading of brain wave activity and the recognition that brain waves were related to mental activity level (including sleep) and neurological malfunctioning (such as brain tumors and epilepsy) spurred sleep research. Modern techniques provided new insights about why we sleep and why we dream. These techniques include **magnetic resonance imaging** (**MRI**), which uses magnetic fields and radio waves to highlight soft areas of the brain, and **positron emission tomography** (**PET**) scans, which use radioactive glucose to show changes that occur as a result of brain activity.

THE BLACK BOX

We do not usually look inside the black boxes—the televisions, tape recorders, cell phones, PDAs, computers, camcorders, and fax machines—that enrich our lives. We cannot see and seldom think about what is going on inside with the microchips, semiconductors, transistors, routers, and fiber electronics—at least, not until they go haywire. Even then, we are likely to replace rather than repair them. It is really not necessary to know about what is going on inside the box, as long as you can turn it on and off.

Your brain is a lot like those black boxes. You use it, value it, stimulate it, and sometimes ignore its messages, but you cannot look inside it. Even if you could be your own neurosurgeon, you would not be able to tell you what your brain cells (**gray matter**) were doing. We can place electrodes on your scalp and record electrical activity in different areas of your brain. After death, we can autopsy the brain and trace the nerve fibers. To gain some understanding of the circuitry, we would need to examine individual brain cells through a powerful microscope. But even this would not reveal what goes on inside the cells. Even with all our technology, the workings of the brain are still a mystery and the interface between brain tissue and thought is still as mysterious as it was four centuries ago, when the French philosopher René Descartes (1596–1650) attempted to explain how the mind and body interact.

Psychologists debate whether we need to look inside the brain to understand behavior. Some feel that we need only study the **stimuli** coming into the brain and the responses of the body to reveal meaningful relationships between the two. Others refuse to ignore the workings of the brain, believing them to be a critical factor in the determination of behavior and personality. In this chapter, we peek inside the brain to explore its relationship to sleep and dreams. We also look at how dreams are built neurologically.

THE SLEEPING BRAIN

Until the beginning of the last century, it was not considered possible to study the sleeping brain. The development of the EEG for studying electrical activity in the brain provided a significant boost to this undertaking by enabling researchers to

Figure 2.1 A patient in a sleep clinic has her brain activity recorded with an electroencephalograph.

obtain brain wave patterns from sleeping subjects (Figure 2.1). Since that time, sleep laboratories have studied the brain waves of thousands of sleeping subjects, revealing vital information about sleep disorders as well as the functioning of the normal brain during sleep.

We now know that sleep is not an all-or-nothing phenomenon; there are levels of sleep, ranging from very light to deep. A sleeper is more easily awakened during the light phases of sleep. There are also individual differences in sleep patterns. Some sleepers are restless, and some sleep "like a log." The stages of sleep and their biological signatures are described later in this chapter.

SLEEP DEFINED

Sleep represents a pronounced physical and psychological change from a waking state. Our eyes roll, our leg muscles twitch, and later, the eyeballs behind our closed lids begin moving rapidly back and forth as dreaming begins. Most significant is the fact that we become oblivious to what is taking place around us. Later, usually when the sun rises, this process is reversed. It does not require sunlight, however, because our biological clock has already been set to wake us at a specific time. As we emerge from sleep, we regain awareness of outside stimuli. We may have a fragmented awareness of what we were dreaming but that usually fades rapidly and we remember nothing of the sleep experience. To a sleeper, it can seem as though the brain was turned off during the sleep process, but this is far from the case. The brain remains active during sleep, although in a very different way. Chemical signals are transmitted throughout

Hamlet's Question

To die, to sleep—
To sleep—perchance, to dream: aye, there's the rub,
For in that sleep of death what dreams may come,
When we have shuffled off this mortal coil,
Must give us pause.

—William Shakespeare (1564–1616)
Hamlet, Act III, Scene I

In this famous speech, Hamlet is talking of death, not sleep, but he makes an association between the two that others have made as well. What is this mysterious thing we call sleep, which some crave, others avoid, scientists study, and poets ponder? Is death a kind of permanent sleep, or is sleep a precursor of death? What of the restorative powers of sleep? Without it, our bodies and minds deteriorate. And what of the dreams that come to all who sleep?

the body to regulate the sleep process. The brain's nerve cells fire, often very rapidly. There is a conscious awareness during dreaming, but it is markedly different from that of the wakened state. Time may be markedly compressed in a dream; what seems like hours may represent only a few seconds in real time (see "Hamlet's Question" box).

HISTORY

Sleep science can trace its origins to 1875 and the discovery by Richard Coton of spontaneous electrical activity in the brains of animals. Another milestone occurred in the 1920s with the German psychiatrist Hans Berger, who discovered that human brains also generated electrical activity that could be recorded using electrical readings from the scalp. Even though Berger had primitive equipment by today's standards, he was able to demonstrate **alpha waves** in wakeful human subjects that disappeared during sleep, to be replaced by low-amplitude waves. Other scientists replicated these findings in the 1930s, but further research was halted by the advent of World War II (1939–1945).

Interest in sleep research surged again in the early 1950s, when improvements in technology made possible more sophisticated investigations of the brain's electrical activity (Figure 2.2). During this time, the notion that sleep was merely the brain turning itself off was itself put permanently to sleep.

Nathaniel Kleitman was the first scientist to devote his research exclusively to sleep. Trained as a physiologist, Kleitman set up a sleep laboratory at the University of Chicago in the 1920s. Kleitman studied the brain activity of volunteers, who slept in a room adjoining his laboratory. Following up on reports that sleep in both infants and adults was accompanied by rolling of the eyeballs just after falling asleep, Kleitman investigated whether such eye movements could be used to measure

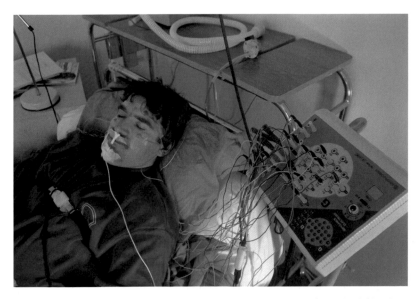

Figure 2.2 In a sleep laboratory, subjects can be monitored while they sleep. This allows scientists to research many different aspects of sleep and dreaming.

the depth of sleep. He assigned a graduate student in physiology, Eugene Aserinsky, to observe the body movements and eye motility of infants. Aserinsky observed 14 infants sleeping during daytime hours and found a regular cycle of body and eye movements every 50 to 60 minutes.

While infants were easier to study, generalization of the findings was limited. Kleitman decided to conduct his investigation in adults as well. Adults, however, presented a more difficult problem. The skin of an infant's eyelid was thin enough to make observation of eye movements relatively easy. This was not true in adults. Furthermore, adult sleep could not be readily observed during the day. Kleitman devised a method of placing electrodes on the eyelids, which enabled him to record eye movements automatically, just as electrical activity is recorded from the brain.

It was while conducting these observations, in 1952, that Aserinsky first noted a new type of rapid eye movement during sleep. This movement was markedly different from the slow movements he had previously observed. When subjects were awakened while experiencing this new rapid eye movement, they reported that they had been dreaming. From this, Kleitman and Aserinsky realized that **REM sleep** was related to dream activity. Around this time, Dr. William Dement joined the research team. The team realized that REM sleep was part of a 90-minute basic sleep cycle. They recognized that it represented a fifth stage of sleep. They also determined that REM sleep was present even in newborn infants. Dement later moved to New York City and established a sleep laboratory at Mount Sinai Hospital. In 1970, Dement founded the world's first sleep disorder center at Stanford University. This was the beginning of sleep medicine.

Dement was also largely responsible for founding the National Center for Sleep Disorders Research under the National Institutes of Health (NIH). In 1999, Dement and Christopher Vaughan collaborated on a book, *The Promise of Sleep*, summarizing sleep research at that time. They established two criteria that identify sleep. The first is that there is a perceptual wall that blocks outside stimuli, which leads to an absence of sensory input. When we sleep, we do not see, hear, or feel most of the sensations generated from things and events outside our bodies. A car passing or a window shade flapping would most likely go unheard. During dreams, however, we receive internal sensations from rapid eye movements and parts of the brain such as the **limbic system** and the **visual cortex**. The second criterion defining sleep is that it is a state that is reversible by intense and persistent outside stimuli. A car backfiring or a loud thunderclap would awaken us. The strange qualities of dreams may arise from the difficulty the brain has in processing eye movement information without the help of visual sensations.

Why We Sleep

One theory of sleep is that it is necessary to consolidate all the information gathered during the waking state. During sleep, the brain seems to be reviewing information that has recently been stored. Deep sleep may weed out certain weak nerve cell connections while strengthening new connections. Studies of rats by Bruce McNaughton, a physiological psychologist at the University of Arizona, showed that the same neurons activated in learning a maze are reactivated during sleep. These findings suggest that the brain may be reviewing recently stored data.

Another theory is that sleep may flush toxic chemical wastes that build up in the brain during the day. Like the rest of the body, the brain runs on the metabolism of glucose. This process produces certain destructive molecules called "free radicals." After 24 hours of wakefulness, the brain loses its ability to use glucose, and brain activity diminishes. Sleep may serve to detoxify those molecules and refresh the brain.

Our Biological Clock

Anyone who has flown cross-country or overseas has experienced jet lag. We may have stayed awake for the entire trip and expected to be very tired when the trip ended. Yet when we land, we feel energized and ready to go. Later, when we want to be doing things, we are suddenly overwhelmed by fatigue and want only to sleep. For the first day or so, we awaken at our old time, even though it is now the middle of the night, and want to go to sleep in the middle of the afternoon. Eventually, we adjust to the new time zone. There is a remarkable mechanism built into our brain that allows us to make this adjustment—an internal clock that becomes conditioned by the daylight to which we are exposed. This internal clock, which is particularly well attuned to the sunrise and sunset of our local surroundings, is a molecular mechanism in our cells that reproduces in our bodies to coincide with the celestial clock based on the rotation of the Earth.

Our biological clock synchronizes a large number of biochemical events in our bodies. Everything we do is in harmony with this internal mechanism. Many people are able to wake up only minutes before their alarm clock goes off. When we travel great distances, our biological clocks account for what seem like inexplicable periods of arousal or drowsiness. The cycles of our biological clock occur even without external sights, sounds, or other time cues. Experiments have revealed that people living in a dark cave follow roughly the same 24-hour sleep/wake cycle they adhered to in a normal environment. They stay awake about 16 hours and sleep about 8 hours. Our internal clock seems to keep us awake during daylight hours, and shuts off during hours of darkness. Bright light continuously resets our biological clock. It is a very powerful time cue. Some studies suggest that even light applied to the back of the leg, not in our eyes, can affect the time mechanism of our bodies. The cycles of our biological clock are called **circadian rhythms.**

In 1972, researchers located the biological clock in two tiny clusters of nerve cells at the midline of our brain, above the optic nerve (the nerve that transmits visual impulses). These nerve cells, called the suprachiasmatic nuclei (SCN), appear to work by means of certain molecules that move in and out of them, like the movements of a clock's pendulum. This finely tuned mechanism at the base of the brain sends a chemical message throughout the body. The closeness of the SCN to these nerve cells allows it to react to light that enters the pupils and to adjust body temperature, hormone levels, and metabolic rate. Thus, the activity of the SCN determines the rhythm of the body's biological clock.

Unfortunately, modern life can disrupt the natural rhythm of our biological clock. Bright lights from incandescent or fluorescent bulbs can act like sunlight, as can television and computer screens. Anecdotal evidence suggests that when people camp out, far removed from the bright lights of the city, they enjoy more natural, uninterrupted, refreshing sleep, although this has not been well established.

By sunrise, there is an increase in **cortisol**, a hormone that usually prepares the body for stress or emergency. Here, it prepares the individual to awaken. In adults, sleep cycles are not smooth, and thus sleep is more disrupted. The schedules of adults are less regular than those of children, and sleep may be affected by medications, alcohol, or caffeine. Most people forget their dreams rapidly, especially those that occur earlier in the sleep cycle. The dream we remember upon awakening is usually the last dream of the night.

It is likely that a circuit in the brain called the **reticular activating system** is responsible for arousal and is therefore an essential mechanism of the biological clock. This system consists of a small number of cells located in the **brain stem**, which is the most primitive part of the brain and is responsible for controlling breathing and other vital bodily processes. The biological clock uses this circuit to wake the brain after sleep and to keep it awake. The reticular activating system releases a number of neurotransmitters—chemical messengers that travel to all the cells of the body—to prepare them to react more rapidly. It also communicates with the **limbic system**, the part of the brain that controls emotions. When the brain is aroused, it responds with a heightened emotional vigilance called the "fight-or-flight" mechanism, which allows us to face challenges or threats. The result of this arousal is a surge of mental and physical energy. There are also neurotransmitters in the brain that act as a brake on the arousal system. They slow the brain down so that it does not act too fast. Alcohol and sleeping pills are two substances that activate this system.

THE STAGES OF SLEEP

Prior to sleep, body temperature begins to decrease slightly. A structure in the brain called the **pineal gland** releases a hormone called **melatonin** into the bloodstream, which prepares the body for sleep. Every 90 to 100 minutes, we pass through a cycle of five distinct sleep stages, each characterized by distinct brain wave patterns (Figure 2.3). The sleep process is studied by analyzing brain waves that reflect the firing of brain cells (neurons). You climb into bed and close your eyes. Your body begins to relax. As you fall asleep, your brain produces slow (8 to 13 per second), high-voltage alpha waves, which are characteristic of calm wakefulness. Breathing rate and brain activity slow further, and the brain produces lower voltage waves. This phase is called Stage 1 sleep. In Stage 1 sleep, alpha waves become less regular, diminish in amplitude, and then disappear. At this point, you lose awareness of the outside world. During Stage 1 sleep, you may experience fantastic images similar to hallucinations. These were called hypnogogic experiences in Chapter 1. You may feel a sense of falling and your leg may jerk. After two to five minutes, Stage 2, a deeper level of sleep, begins. Stage 2 sleep consists of rapid (13 to 16 per second), rhythmic waves known as **sleep spindles**, which last two to three minutes. Garbled, often nonsensical, sleep talking may occur in this stage. There are occasional rises and falls of the amplitude (wave height) of the entire EEG. After another 20 minutes, you enter Stage 3 sleep, a much deeper level that consists of low-frequency, high-voltage **delta waves**. Delta waves look larger and more regular, like waves in the ocean. A sleeper is much harder to arouse at this time. Stage 4, the deepest level, also consists of slow delta waves that occur almost constantly. Delta waves last about 20 minutes. Sleepwalking, when it occurs, happens during Stage 4. Although low-level noise, such as a car passing, does not generally disturb sleep, loud noises or certain specific sounds, such as a

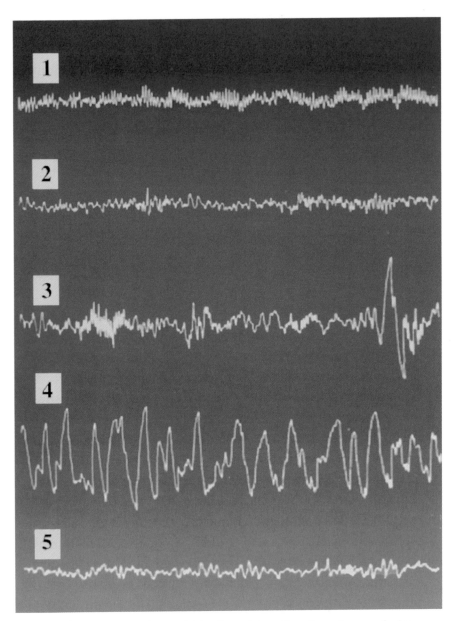

Figure 2.3 Encephalograph tracings show the five stages of sleep. Stage 1, at the top, shows alpha waves, which occur as we lose awareness of the outside world. By Stage 3, the EEG shows large delta waves, which become regular in Stage 4 sleep. Stage 5 represents REM sleep, when dreams occur. The patterns shown in Stage 5 are similar to those of Stage 1.

baby crying or a familiar name, can stimulate the auditory cortex of the brain.

Children have a different sleep biology from adults. During Stage 4 sleep, a child's body releases a growth hormone, which facilitates cell division and repair. During puberty, the body also releases prolactin, another hormone, whose purpose during sleep in unknown. Bedwetting in children occurs during Stage 4.

A dramatic change was first observed by Kleitman and Aserinsky at Stanford University in 1953. They noted that after about an hour of sleep, the sleeper's eyes began moving back and forth, while their EEG patterns shifted from deep sleep to a pattern more characteristic of Stage 1 sleep. Delta waves disappeared. During this time, the subject's breathing also became irregular. Subjects awakened at these times reported that they had been dreaming. This phase of sleep, Stage 5, now associated with dreaming, is called rapid eye movement (REM) sleep. It occurs periodically throughout the night. It was also discovered that during REM sleep a dreamer's muscles are paralyzed. The muscles lose their tension and become totally relaxed, effectively immobilizing the sleeper. REM sleep is also known as paradoxical sleep since it seems unusual that while we are dreaming of moving, our muscles are immobilized (see "REM Paralysis" box).

REM sleep lasts about 10 minutes, after which the individual descends once again into Stages 3 and 4. This pattern repeats and the sleeper may enter REM sleep again after about 90 minutes. This cycle may occur four to six times a night. Each time, REM sleep follows Stage 4 sleep. There may be a series of ups and downs and several dreaming episodes during the night. Deepest sleep is achieved during the first half of the night. REM sleep increases in frequency and duration during the second half of the night.

Brain waves are very different in REM sleep and non-REM sleep. When we are asleep and not dreaming, brain waves are synchronous. This means that groups of brain cells are firing together. This is very different from what happens when we are awake. The waking brain fires in an asynchronous manner; that is, individual brain cells fire individually as they transmit and process information. During REM sleep—that is, during dreaming—brain waves resemble those characteristic of an awakened state.

DREAM FORMATION

Current understanding of dream formation is that the images and thought processes of dreaming are modifications of thought processes that occur during wakefulness. This suggests that the same parts of the brain that determine our thinking when we are awake are also active when we are asleep. It has been shown that during dreaming, the part of the brain responsible for vision—the visual cortex—is also firing. Presumably, this is what produces the visual imagery of dreams. But there is one big difference: Without external stimulation, the brain has no sense of time. It can produce images in space but without an accurate

REM Paralysis

The onset of REM sleep is associated with more than dreaming. The body becomes rigid with a paralysis of the voluntary muscles. Nerve messages from the brain to the brain stem inhibit the activity of motor neurons in the spinal cord. This paralysis continues through REM sleep and sometimes slightly after. If this did not occur, the dreamer would act out his or her dream. In some cases, REM paralysis can be overcome, presumably when there is strong motivation or emotion. The sleeper may suddenly jerk his or her limbs or mumble. The heart and lungs are not paralyzed. These effects are produced by the autonomic nervous system, which controls involuntary muscles.

time sequence. That is why some dreams seem like they take hours, when REM brain waves indicate that only seconds have passed. The rich imagery in dreams has to depend on memory and learned associations. Our past history with apples, for example, includes qualities of redness or greenness, roundness, and sweetness or sourness. Sometimes our associations are irrelevant, adding to the bizarre nature of dreams. Interestingly, Freud's method of free association required that the patient close his or her eyes to reduce outside stimulation.

Other parts of the brain also contribute to the dreaming process. The limbic system lies at the innermost edge of the **cerebral hemispheres**. One part of the limbic system is the **hippocampus**, which is instrumental in storing memories. Without the hippocampus, short-term memory would remain short term, as if someone forgot to hit the "save" button on a computer. During REM sleep, certain cells in the brain stem produce another brain wave pattern—theta rhythm, which is necessary for memory processing in the hippocampus. If movement of the body is occurring, the brain stem cannot produce theta rhythms. Presumably, for this reason, the body is paralyzed except for eye movements, which do not interfere with theta rhythms. Information from memory is reprocessed during REM sleep and provides much of the content for dreams. In this way, our memory reactivates thoughts relating to self-image, fears, insecurity, strengths, wishes, jealousy, and love. The emotions associated with these thoughts are activated by the limbic system.

A NEED FOR DREAMS

If sleeping subjects are awakened every 30 minutes (before the onset of REM), they will go through early sleep stages rapidly and soon begin REM sleep. This was an unexpected finding, since it is logical to assume that someone with severe sleep deprivation requires deeper sleep (Stages 3 and 4) rather than the lighter REM sleep. This finding implies that not only is there a strong need for sleep in sleep-deprived individuals, but, specifically, there is a need for REM sleep. Does this also imply a need for dreaming? People who are deprived of sleep for many days have reported auditory and visual hallucinations. One theory is that sleep is a kind of nighttime psychosis that ensures daytime emotional stability. This has not been established and there is no evidence that deprivation of REM sleep causes mental illness. While unproven, it is not unreasonable to assume that dream deprivation can have psychological consequences.

While psychoanalysts still endorse psychoanalytic theory about the wish-fulfilling function of dreams, some psychologists suggest alternative reasons for dreaming. One theory is that dreams serve an information-processing function. They assume that dreams are attempts to integrate recently gained knowledge with past memories. They dispute the idea that dreams have a specific intent or message. Dreams do not contain hidden meanings. They do represent reality, although in a distorted way, and in this sense, dreams are meaningful. They can provide a picture of the personality of the dreamer. Dream content should not be taken at face value, however, but rather as the simplest way for the dreamer to express some idea while asleep.

A physiological theory of dreaming proposed in 1987 by Martin Seligman, a psychologist at the University of Pennsylvania, is that dreams, or REM sleep, provide the brain with stimulation that is required to develop and preserve the brain's nerve pathways. This theory is supported by the fact that infants, whose brains are rapidly developing, spend most of their time in REM sleep. We have already mentioned theories stating that dreams are the brain's attempt to sort through the stimulation coming from the visual cortex and limbic system, without additional information coming from external sources. If this mechanism provides a purpose for dreams, it relates to brain function, not unconscious motivation.

■ **Learn more about the biology of sleep** Search the Internet for *sleeping brain*, *REM sleep*, and *circadian rhythm*.

3 Insomnia and Sleep Disorders

Sleep problems arise from many sources: sleep deprivation, malfunctioning of the biological clock, stress, environmental conditions, injury, and physical or mental illness. Sleep problems may last one night or a lifetime. The most common sleep problems are insomnia, sleepwalking, and night terrors.

INSOMNIA

Insomnia is an inability to sleep normally. It can last weeks or years. It may be intermittent, lasting a few nights, improving, and later returning. Insomnia is not a specific sleep disorder, since it may have many different causes, but rather is a sign of a larger problem. People with insomnia cannot easily fall asleep. They sleep shorter hours and awaken well before normal rising time. In one large study of adults, 6% of males and 14% of females reported that they had problems falling asleep or staying asleep at night and were tired during the day. Insomnia seems to be a problem that is unique to humans. Cats and dogs show no signs of insomnia. People tend to overestimate the time they stay awake at night, often confusing light sleep or restless sleep with wakefulness. They tend to remember time spent awake, since they have no memory of being asleep. Frequent causes of insomnia are worry, depression, and anxiety. Certain drugs such as caffeine and other stimulants may interfere with sleep. Alcohol can result in more rapid onset of sleep, but it also interferes with normal sleep patterns and REM sleep. Even sleep medications may disturb normal sleep and are not prescribed over a long period of time. People with insomnia experience racing and uncontrollable thoughts. Other causes of insomnia include:

- Restless legs syndrome (RLS; see "Restless Legs Syndrome" box), which is characterized by uncontrolled leg movements.
- Gastroesophageal reflux, the flow of stomach acid into the esophagus.
- Fibromyalgia, pain in certain muscles and tendons, accompanied by fatigue.
- Emotional or psychiatric problems.

Treating insomnia is difficult. There are no miracle cures; claims that people can be easily cured in a short period of time

Restless Legs Syndrome

In 1998, a poll conducted by the National Sleep Foundation identified restless legs syndrome (RLS) as a major cause of insomnia. Many physicians are not aware of this condition, so it remains largely undiagnosed. The symptom consists of persistent, uncontrollable, uncomfortable, and sometimes painful feelings in the legs that produce a desire to move them. This symptom disturbs sleep and may make it difficult to fall asleep. The basic cause of RLS is unknown. The prevalence of RLS is also unknown, but conservative estimates of 5% of the population would mean there are 10 million sufferers in the United States.

are misleading. William C. Dement and Christopher Vaughan list five strategies that have proven helpful: improving sleep hygiene, using relaxation techniques, controlling outside stimuli, changing inappropriate thoughts, and regulating sleep time. Sleep hygiene includes things such as keeping a regular schedule, avoiding caffeine before bedtime, and making sure the bedroom or sleep area is properly ventilated. Relaxation techniques are used by behavior therapists to help patients deal with stress and anxiety disorders. They involve muscle relaxation and breathing exercises. Stimulus control refers to the avoidance of stimulating or unpleasant activities just before bedtime. For some people, watching the 11:00 P.M. news can be upsetting. Paying bills, doing homework, and answering e-mail can also increase anxiety levels before bedtime. Worrying about problems or planning tasks for the next day is not conducive to sleep. Cognitive techniques include the practice of simple, repetitive thoughts that occupy the mind effortlessly and prevent preoccupation with worries or concerns. Counting sheep is an age-old method. Repeated calculation, such as starting with 1,000 and subtracting sevens consecutively, is another. Sleep state restriction is a controlled method of manipulating the amount of time devoted to sleep. People with insomnia may be advised to allow only four hours for sleep initially. Gradually, another half an hour may be added until the individual builds up to a normal eight-hour sleep schedule. Other sleep-inducing strategies include hypnosis, meditation, acupuncture, acupressure, massage, herbal teas, warm milk, and prescription sleeping pills. Many people resist taking sleeping pills for fear of becoming addicted to them. Physicians may avoid prescribing them for the same reason. Some sleep medications have serious side effects. Certain medications that depress the nervous system can cause unconsciousness and even death. In the 1970s, physicians began prescribing benzodiazapines such as Valium® and Librium® for sleep. These drugs were originally developed to treat anxiety but were found to induce sleep and were far safer than earlier drugs used for that purpose. Barbiturates were also used to safely induce sleep. Today, a new class of hypnotic medications (imidazopyridines), which includes the drug Ambien®, has proven to be an effective, nonaddictive sleep aid. Benzodiazepines, barbiturates, and imidazopyridines all act on a receptor in the brain that inhibits nervous activity. Despite the effectiveness of these drugs, many physicians are still concerned about safety or abuse and remain reluctant or unwilling to prescribe them. Some people buy over-the-counter sleep aids, which have no proven effectiveness.

SLEEPWALKING

Sleepwalking is a condition in which a person who is asleep walks around and even performs activities but is not in a waking state (Figure 3.1). Sleepwalking does not occur during dreaming. Since muscles are usually paralyzed during REM sleep, sleepwalking would not generally be possible while a person is dreaming. Sleepwalking usually occurs during Stages 3 or 4 of sleep, several hours after going to bed. There is no known treatment; the only safeguard is to lock doors and windows. During the sleepwalking episode, the individual seems to stare blankly and does not respond to communication. It is possible, though difficult, to awaken a sleepwalker. Because it can be traumatic for the sleepwalker to be awakened, the best course of action is to guide the person back to bed. The next morning, the sleepwalker will have no memory of the sleepwalking event.

NIGHT TERRORS

Children and occasionally adults experience **night terrors**. The person, while asleep, may suddenly sit up or walk around. According to a 1981 report, heart rate and breathing increase. The person

Figure 3.1 In this time-lapse image, a young woman leaves her bed. Sleepwalking does not occur while dreaming since the muscles are paralyzed during REM sleep.

appears terrified. Usually, the person does not fully awaken and does not remember the incident the next morning. Night terrors are not nightmares, which usually occur in the early morning hours during REM sleep. Like sleepwalking, night terrors occur within the first few hours of sleep, during Stage 4 of the sleep cycle.

SNORING

Snoring is considered a sleep disorder since it involves an impairment of breathing during sleep. We breathe through a stiff tube called the trachea, which is formed in such a way that it does not collapse when we suck air inward. The rigidity of the throat is achieved in part by muscle tension. When we fall asleep, these throat muscles relax. When we inhale during sleep, the walls of the throat are pulled inward. As we exhale, the throat walls rebound. This breathing cycle sets up a vibration of the throat wall that creates the sound of snoring (Figure 3.2). In healthy sleepers, this vibration is not strong enough to cause snoring. In loud snorers, however, the throat is almost entirely blocked, so that not enough air enters the lungs. In extreme cases, snoring can cause apnea or an awakening due to lack of air.

SLEEP APNEA

Sleep apnea is when a person stops breathing during sleep. The breathing interruption can last from 10 to 40 seconds and is usually followed by snorting and, usually, awakening. The National Heart, Lung, and Blood Institute estimates that one in 25 people may suffer from sleep apnea. Overweight men are the most likely to be affected. After a few moments of not breathing, the oxygen level in the blood is depleted, which causes the sleeper to awaken and gulp air. The process may repeat as many as 400 times a night. Often, the individual is unaware that he or she suffers from this condition. People with sleep apnea may be deprived of slow wave sleep and may feel chronically tired and irritable. Severe cases are treated by the insertion of a breathing cylinder into the trachea. The cylinder can be closed off during waking hours. Risk factors for sleep apnea include enlarged tonsils and lymph nodes, obesity, and a small airway. Sleep apnea is sometimes successfully treated by surgical procedures that cut away or use laser beams to remove excess tissue at the back of the throat. Another approach is to use a mask that blows air into the nose at a slightly higher pressure than the surrounding air pressure. The increased air pressure maintains an open air passage. Dental devices can also

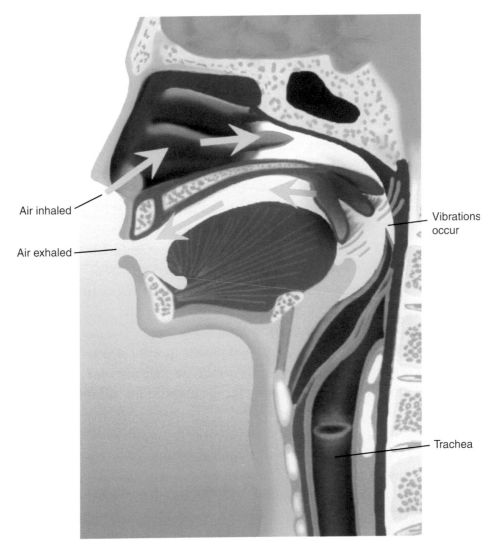

Air inhaled

Air exhaled

Vibrations occur

Trachea

Figure 3.2 Snoring occurs when the throat muscles relax during sleep and is considered a sleep disorder. As the snorer breathes, the throat wall is pulled in with each inhalation and rebounds with each exhalation. This vibration creates the sounds which we refer to as snoring. Snoring has been known to cause apnea in extreme cases.

sometimes be used to move the lower jaw forward. Sleep apnea has been linked to **sudden infant death syndrome** (SIDS), a condition in which apparently healthy babies are placed in their cribs and are later found dead. Parents are urged to allow infants to sleep only on their backs, a practice that has greatly reduced the incidence of SIDS. One treatment for sleep apnea is the use of a special respirator over the face that blows air at a steady pressure to keep the individual breathing regularly.

NARCOLEPSY

Narcolepsy is a serious condition that consists of a sudden, irresistible urge to sleep. The word *narcolepsy* is derived from the Greek words *narco,* which means "numbness," and *lepsy,* which means "seizure." Narcolepsy can strike a person at any time— during sports, when driving, or while operating dangerous machinery. As with REM sleep, a person with narcolepsy may experience vivid images and a loss of muscle tone. Sometimes the person "sees" a strange light. In narcolepsy, REM sleep occurs suddenly, without the usual passage through the lighter stages of sleep. The visual images associated with narcolepsy are one possible explanation for the accounts offered by people who claim to have been abducted by aliens. One form of narcolepsy involves the onset of muscle weakness or almost total paralysis that may last for a few seconds to several minutes. The individual may collapse into a chair or onto the floor. According to the National Commission on Sleep Disorder Research, one person in 1,000 is affected. Narcolepsy is treated with stimulant medication, such as amphetamines and Ritalin®, and restriction of activities such as driving or using dangerous machinery. The goal of treatment is to provide a reasonable degree of alertness to allow the person to attend school or to work and to drive short distances. Just as insulin does not cure diabetes, but replaces what is missing, stimulants do not cure narcolepsy. There is no known cure for narcolepsy.

William Dement has been an outspoken advocate for sleep research and treatment. Our sleep, he points out, is fragile. Various surveys suggest that as much as 50% of the population is sleep deprived. A lack of sleep is the cause of untold unhappiness, illness, and automobile, airplane, and boating accidents. Yet, unfortunately, many people do not regard sleep as significant, and it has never been considered a health priority by medical authorities, including those that run large federal funding agencies.

■ **Learn more about sleep disorders** Search the Internet for *insomnia, night terrors*, and *narcolepsy*.

4 | Sleep Research

SLEEP DEPRIVATION AND SLEEP DEBT

Sleep researchers generally accept that the amount of time it takes to fall asleep is directly related to the amount of time one has gone without sleep. The less sleep a person has had, the easier it is for him or her to fall asleep. We require about one hour of sleep for every two hours we spend awake, or about eight hours of sleep a night. Becoming aroused—for example, by participating in sports or driving a car—is often enough to make us believe we are no longer sleepy. That feeling is really an illusion. As soon as the arousal period is over, a strong feeling of sleepiness sets in. Sleep loss does not go away; it accumulates. It is a debt that eventually must be paid back. Serious accidents have been attributed to long-term sleep loss.

In Chapter 2, we saw how the biological clock is largely a function of external light conditions. When we change time zones, we experience a period of adjustment until our circadian rhythms readjust to the new light schedule. The biological clock is not entirely dependent upon external stimulation, however. Nathaniel Kleitman conducted research to determine whether circadian rhythms could be modified. In

1938, he and a colleague arranged to spend one month in the Mammoth Cave in Kentucky. The idea was to completely isolate themselves from external stimulation. They scheduled themselves to live a 28-hour day. During their waking hours, they spent their time recording their temperature and motility. Kleitman's colleague adjusted very well to the new time schedule. He slept nine hours and his temperature and motility followed the new schedule easily. Kleitman himself, however, could not adjust to the 28-hour schedule. His temperature and movements continued to follow a 24-hour schedule. Had both men responded like Kleitman, they might have concluded that the 24-hour biological clock was unchangeable. Because one researcher easily adjusted to the 28-hour schedule, Kleitman concluded that there is no inborn mechanism that has hardwired us to follow a 24-hour day.

A more controlled experiment was performed in 1961 at the Max Plank Institute in Germany. Researchers built an underground environment that completely obscured all signs that would reveal the time of day. External light and sounds were removed. The room was shielded from changing external electromagnetic fields that would have affected brain wave readings. The research assistants even shaved at varying times during the day to avoid providing clues from their "five o'clock shadow." The subjects were allowed to make their own schedule—turning lights on when they wanted to be awake and turning them off when they wanted to sleep. Interestingly, the subjects soon settled into a 25-hour day. They went to sleep and woke up a little later each day until their days were no longer synchronized with external time. When they finally emerged from underground, more time had passed than they realized. This slightly longer biological day may account for the common experience of feeling tired on Monday morning. Our biological clock seems to demand a few more hours.

The sleep debt we accumulate works as a separate process. As we accumulate sleep debt, we build a need that must be met. In such circumstances, sleep deprivation may work in opposition to the biological clock. William Dement and Christopher Vaughan suggested a possible explanation of these effects. They believe that there is a need to maintain a zero sleep debt. If we go without sleep, the tendency to want to sleep increases. If we sleep too much, the tendency to remain awake increases.

Sleep deprivation does more than make us tired. A growing body of evidence indicates that it is detrimental to health. A study reported in *Nature* suggests that serious impairments of brain function are associated with sleep deprivation. A team of researchers at the University of California, San Diego, and the San Diego Veterans Administration Hospital monitored the brain activity of subjects while they performed simple verbal learning tasks. In one study, 13 normal, active subjects were evaluated in a sleep laboratory to determine their normal sleep patterns. They were then kept awake for 35 hours and asked to perform certain cognitive tasks. MRI scans were performed during this time, producing images that revealed activity in various parts of their brains. Researchers compared the subjects' activity in the rested state through increasing stages of sleep deprivation. The studies indicated that the brain is dynamic in its efforts to deal with sleep deprivation. Both increased and decreased activation of various regions of the brain were observed. The overall effect upon performance, however, was detrimental. The effects also differed on the basis of the specific cognitive task that the individual was asked to perform.

The prefrontal cortex, the area of the brain associated with planning and problem solving, was more active when subjects were sleepy. Similarly, the parietal lobe was more active in sleepy subjects than in rested subjects during the learning task.

On the other hand, the temporal lobe (the area associated with language processing) was active during verbal learning in rested subjects but not in sleep-deprived subjects. Areas of the brain that were active in rested subjects who were working on arithmetic problems were not active in sleep-deprived subjects. No other part of the brain took over. Subjects who were sleepy had fewer correct answers and skipped more problems. This is significant because students and workers are often pushed to perform when they are sleep-deprived.

SLEEP AND AGING

Sleep begins before birth. The sleeping fetus is very active, as any pregnant mother can verify. Even so, the human fetus sleeps 16 to 20 hours a day. Half of that sleep time is taken up by REM sleep. This compares with about 25% for adults. By age 65, REM sleep is only about 15% to 20%. The fetus even demonstrates circadian rhythm, even though it is not being stimulated by light. The mechanism is the chemical messages (melatonin) it receives through the bloodstream of the mother.

By the time of his or her first birthday, a baby still sleeps about 15 hours a day. Sleep time reduces with age so that the toddler at 18 months is taking only one nap during the day. The two-year-old usually sleeps about 50% of the time. From ages two to five, sleep is reduced to about ten hours a day. Teenagers usually need as much sleep as younger children, but they often fail to get it. In adolescence, sleep time begins to decline further. Social activities and increasing independence place limitations upon sleep, as the adolescent finds ways to stay up later at night. In one survey, only 5% of teenagers said that their parents still set bedtime limits on them. This trend only gets worse with young adults, over 50% of whom indicate that they feel drowsy during the day. Many report that they often drive while they are sleepy. During middle age, the average person sleeps about eight hours a day. It is possible that there is now less of a need for sleep. For people of retirement age (65 and above), the frequency of sleep disorders increases. Sleep becomes more fragmented. Older people wake up several times at night, often to go to the bathroom. In very old age (80 and above), people sleep a great deal of time.

Most non-REM, slow-wave sleep occurs during the first three hours of sleep. Children experience the highest percentage of slow-wave sleep. As we age, we spend less time in slow-wave sleep, which accounts for sleep being more fitful in adults.

SLEEP, THE IMMUNE SYSTEM, AND LONGEVITY

Our bodies are equipped to fight off bacteria, viruses, protozoa, and fungi that can cause disease. Our skin, nasal mucus, stomach acid, antibodies, and immune cells all participate in the fight against foreign organisms that enter the body. The immune system, however, can be compromised in many ways and by many invaders. The most devastating is the human immunodeficiency virus (HIV), the organism that causes acquired immunodeficiency syndrome (AIDS). Sleep is an important component in keeping the immune system intact.

A large body of evidence links sleep patterns to health and long life. It has yet to be proven, however, that people who sleep more live longer and that those who sleep less are more prone to die earlier. A study of more than one million people undertaken by the American Cancer Society in 1950 found that the highest mortality rate occurred among people who slept fewer than four hours a day, as well as those who slept nine hours a day or more. The lowest mortality rate was found among people who habitually slept about eight hours a day. A similar study of 1,000 adults in Finland found that males who have trouble sleeping were 6.5

times more likely to have a variety of health problems than those without sleep problems. Females with poor sleep patterns were 3.5 times more likely to have health problems than their counterparts. Increasing evidence suggests that sleep is necessary to maintain a healthy immune system by sustaining the activity of certain immune cells and chemicals. In both children and adults, growth hormone is released during sleep to repair damaged body cells and to build new cells.

There is also evidence that getting too much sleep may also be related to shorter life span. This finding is not completely understood. It may be that people in both the short- and long-sleeper groups are those who have terminal illnesses or sleep disorders such as sleep apnea. These people may not really be long sleepers, but rather those who spend log hours in bed alternating between sleep and wakefulness. The greatest longevity is found in those who regularly sleep eight-hour days. These data illustrate that a correlation between two variables does not demonstrate causality. Other factors may be involved.

BRAIN AREAS AND DREAMS

A study by University of Pennsylvania psychologists Martin Seligman and Amy Yellen in 1987 found that bursts of rapid eye movements during sleep coincided with bursts of activity in the visual cortex. Contradictory evidence was provided by a 1997 study at the NIH led by Allen Braun and Thomas J. Balkin. These workers used PET scans to map the human brain during REM sleep. A radioactive glucose solution was injected into the brain to make blood flow visible. Blood flow is an index of nervous system activity. In the PET scans, active areas of the brain appear lighted, whereas inactive areas remain dark. The study revealed that the visual cortex, as well as the areas used to process sensory information, was inactive. The most active areas were those dealing with emotion (limbic system) and old memories (hippocampus). PET scan readings, however, have relatively low resolution, so that lower levels of activity in the visual cortex would not be detected.

SLEEP AND MOOD

Sleep deprivation is also directly related to feelings of irritability, frustration, and unhappiness. Sleepiness interferes with social relationships. It results in symptoms such as headache, stomachache, and joint and muscular pains. Good sleep, on the other hand, is associated with good feelings, happiness, and vitality. David Dinges and his coworkers at the University of Pennsylvania limited subjects to four hours a day of sleep for a week. He asked subjects to take many performance tests and to respond to measures of their mood and feelings. They were rated on the degree of happiness or unhappiness, calmness or stress, energy or fatigue, and also asked to indicate any physical symptoms they were experiencing. The results clearly revealed that people who were in sleep debt felt less happy, more physically challenged, and more mentally and physically exhausted. These mood indicators increased negatively as sleep deprivation increased. Mood scores bounced back in a positive direction when subjects were allowed to sleep enough to erase their sleep debt.

RECENT WORK

The most exciting studies in sleep research are so recent that conclusions are still tentative. Much of this work has yet to appear in textbooks. A 2004 issue of *Time* magazine summarizes some ongoing studies that provide new hypotheses about the purpose of sleep. Ongoing studies at the Weitzman Institute in Rehovot, Israel, are focusing on specific types of memory that may be affected by sleep.

Procedural memory refers to the learning of tasks that require practice and repetition, like learning to type a sequence of numbers. This is a different memory process from learning the names of the capitals of each state. Robert Strickland, a neuroscientist at Harvard Medical School and Matthew Walker at Beth Israel Deaconess Medical Center tested the effects of sleep on procedural memory in learning to type the numbers 4-1-2-3-4 with the left hand. No matter when the subjects learned the task, their accuracy improved 60% to 70% after six minutes of practice. The subjects who learned the task in the morning and were tested 12 hours later did not improve significantly beyond this. Subjects who were taught the task in the evening and tested again after a night's sleep improved 15% to 20% in speed and 30% to 40% in accuracy. Those who improved the most had spent the most time in non-REM (deep) sleep. Other procedural tasks seemed to require both REM and non-REM sleep.

These results suggest that different types of tasks may require different types of sleep. Studies of the firing of individual neurons in rats by Bruce McNaughton at the University of Arizona found that the same brain neurons used to learn a maze during waking hours are reactivated at night during REM sleep. McNaughton suggested that during REM sleep, the brain is reviewing recently stored information. It may be, then, that the purpose of sleep is to strengthen newly learned brain connections without losing older connections.

Contrary to the Freudian idea that dreams originate from wishes, Professor Allan Hobson of the Sleep Research Laboratory of Cornell University's Psychology Department believes that dreams come from spontaneous neural activity of the brainstem. Nonrandom waves of neural activity in the retina identified by researchers at Harvard University are thought to correspond with eye movements during REM sleep. These waves are believed to stabilize changes in the nerve conductivity that is known to accompany learning. The amount of time spent in REM sleep correlates with certain types of learning, such as the learning of spatial configurations. The implication is that these retinal waves affect memory consolidation. This is speculative, however, since it has not been shown that retinal waves actually change the structure of neurons in humans. Research at MIT with rats has demonstrated that neural learning circuits replay in the hippocampus during REM sleep. It is hypothesized that the hippocampus in humans is responsible for

Dreams as Physiological Product

The advent of modern electrophysiological recording technology led some sleep researchers to suggest that the origin of dreams was physiological, not psychological. Allan Hobson and Robert McCarley took the position that dreams are the result of spontaneous firing of neurons of the pons, a brain structure near the cerebellum. Dreams have no motivational meaning, they assert. Stimulation from the pons speads to the forebrain, which synthesizes this data into a dream. Analyzing 100 dreams obtained after waking subjects from REM sleep, they found that a large proportion of dream content referred to movements of the lower extremities. This would be expected if dreams originated in the pons. This theory has been criticized as an oversimplification and remains controversial. It ignores a great deal of psychological evidence that dreams reflect individual personality variables such as anxiety, conflict, guilt, and daily concerns. The answer may prove as irresolvable as the proverbial chicken-or-the-egg question.

Source: Hobson, J. A., and R. W. McCarley. "The Brain as a Dream State Generator: An Activation-synthesis Hypothesis of the Dream Process." *American Journal of Psychiatry* 134 (1977): 1335–1348.

the linking of people, places, persons, objects, actions, and time. These findings have been used to support the view that REM sleep consolidates memory in humans, a theory that has been criticized because of the bizarre and disorganized nature of dreams. How can such a disordered process account for memory, which is so organized? One possibility is that the re-play of neural circuits in the hippocampus may still contribute to dreams, but other factors are also likely involved. Dreams may be confused because of the reduced activity of the **neocortex** during sleep and the absence of external stimulation. This re-sults in a kind of **dementia**. The neocortex does not respond to the bizarre and illogical quality of the dream. These findings are tentative and still controversial. They represent the vanguard of research that uses the newest technology to determine the real purpose of sleep and dreaming.

So far, we have concentrated on the biology of sleep and dreams. Were this the entire story, our book would end here. The focus now shifts away from the physiological underpinnings of sleep and dreams and turns to the purely subjective charac-teristics—specifically, dreaming (see "Dreams as Physiological Product" box).

■ **Learn more about sleep research** Search the Internet for *Nathaniel Kleitman* and *sleep deprivation.*

5 | Everyone Dreams

Now Allah has created the dream not only as a means of guidance and instruction, I refer to the dream, but He has also made it a window on the universe.

Prophet Muhammad, 7th century A.D.

You approach the diving board. You are the last diver and your team is behind. If you do a perfect dive, your team will win the gold. You are climbing the ladder, but the steps are missing. All eyes are on you. You pull yourself up with your arms. Finally, you reach the top, but now you are exhausted. You look down and the pool is empty. You must jump, but your legs have turned to Jell-O®. You cannot climb back down because the ladder has disappeared. Suddenly, your math teacher is on the diving board with you and is pushing you off. You feel yourself falling, but now you are flying. Your math homework is in your hands. You let go and the pages are fluttering down. You must retrieve them or you will flunk algebra. Your mother is flying next to you, pushing a spoonful of Cheerios® into your mouth.

You sit up in bed, trembling. Your heart is racing. OK, it was just a dream. How weird! You try to recall it but the images are gone. You know it was scary. Your stomach is doing somersaults. Oh, no, you think. Will I ever survive this day? I should have studied for that math test instead of watching the Olympics on TV. I'll get my notes together and study in homeroom. No time for breakfast. . . .

How do we explain dreams? Is there some dream atlas in which we can find the meaning of specific actions and images, like diving and flying? You can find such books in the library, your favorite bookstore, or on the Internet. They might explain that dreams of flying are common and that they signify a desire for independence or escape—a common concern of teenagers. You might find other elements from your dream—well, maybe not Cheerios—and then be able to put together an interpretation of the dream's meaning. However, would the author of the dream atlas know that you had a math test that morning or that you would like to push your teacher off the diving board or that your mother bugs you about eating a good breakfast every morning?

Even people who deny that they dream exhibit brain wave patterns that indicate dreaming activity. For some, dreams are vivid and exciting; for others, they may be frightening. We awaken with a dream fresh in our minds but, unless we immediately make a concerted effort to recall it or write it down, it disappears within seconds. It is gone forever, as if someone pressed the "delete" button. Dreams that we do recall are often fragmented and bizarre. We find ourselves doing things that make little sense. The people we dream about are often familiar to us—family, friends, teachers, and neighbors. Yet, they are often engaged in activities that are not typical. They may say or do things that are more characteristic of someone else we know. The dream sequence may be jumbled, nonsensical, irrational, and illogical. We solve problems that seem brilliant in the dream, but ridiculous when we wake up.

ANCIENT AND CLASSICAL THINKING ABOUT DREAMS

Despite their seemingly nonsensical nature, or perhaps because of it, dreams have fascinated people throughout history. The Bible describes the use of dreams in prophecy. Joseph interpreted the pharaoh's dream to make a place for himself at court. The ability to foresee the future in dreams is still accepted in many cultures. Researchers study the dream process in the laboratory, attempting to locate the dream process in brain activity.

* * *

You, Yorg, are of prehistoric times. At age 14, you are soon to assume your duties as a hunter. Before the initiation ritual in which you will become a man, you must spend three nights alone on a distant mountain. Each night, you will eat a sacred root so that your spirit will leave your body to wander the Earth. You will be purified by this experience, which will bring much wisdom. You worry about whether you will be up to the task and whether your spirit will find its way back to your body. If you are worthy, the Great Spirit will assist you in your journey. If you fail in this endeavor, you will join the ranks of the living dead and wander the universe forever.

* * *

You are Josephine, daughter to the king of Mesopotamia. You are admired for your beauty and your wit, but most of all, for your gift of prophecy. Your father's subjects come to you with their dreams. You are revered for your forecast of the great drought. Your wisdom has saved the people from famine. You know dreams are messages from the gods. They reveal one's personal destiny. Dreams of storms reveal approaching evil or misfortune. Some dreams are so dangerous that they must not be spoken.

* * *

You are Merriah, of 15th-century Madrid. You are thought to be a witch who communicates with demons through dreams. You are to be examined by the torturers of the Inquisition. You are to be stretched out on the rack until you confess your sins. The priest Tomás de Torquemada, known for his cruelty, will question you. There is no escape.

*   *   *

Ancient philosophers believed that dreams were divinely inspired, that they were messages from the gods, not of the body (see "Aristotle on Dreams" box). This idea is a central philosophical issue that has intrigued the great thinkers and scientists of history. Those who make a rigid distinction between mind and body are

Aristotle on Dreams

Hundreds of years before the birth of Jesus, wise men in Greece began to think about the reasons for everything that goes on in the world, including why people think and act as they do. Unlike his teacher Plato, who drew sharp distinctions between soul (mind) and body, Aristotle (384–322 B.C.) believed that mind was a process of the body. His legacy to science was his insistence upon the use of natural observation in describing human experience and behavior.

Earlier thinkers believed dreams to be of divine origin. They distinguished between true dreams, sent to the dreamer as warnings or to foretell the future, and fraudulent dreams, whose object was to mislead the person. Aristotle believed that dreams are not divine or supernatural, but subject to natural laws. He saw dreams as the result of the mental activity of the dreamer. He believed that dreams convert slight sensations into intense sensation. If someone felt warm, he would dream he was walking through fire. Over 1,600 years since the death of Aristotle, there are still people who believe that dreams have the mystical power to tell the future.

called dualists. The Greek philosopher Plato (427–347 B.C.) believed that only the mind, being immaterial, could understand the ideal world of thought, reason, and abstraction. The mind survives after death. It can **transcend** the concrete and immediate properties of physical objects. Philosophers also must be mathematicians, Plato reasoned, to deal with abstract relationships that are more real than the world of the senses.

The 17th-century French philosopher René Descartes (1596–1650) attempted to explain how an immaterial soul could interact with a material body. Anatomists had dissected the human body and identified a tiny "pineal" body at the midpoint of the brain. Its function was unknown. Descartes suggested that the spirit and body interacted at this site, since it occupies a central anatomical position. The functioning of the pineal gland is still not completely understood. It is known that the pineal gland works in conjunction with the suprachiasmatic nucleus (SCN), is a light sensitive organ, is related to the production of melatonin, and is part of the brain's time-keeping mechanism. The major religions of the world accept the idea that the soul leaves the body at death. Even today, there are people who believe that the spirit can exit the body during sleep and travel the world. Dreams have intrigued philosophers since ancient times, but it was not until the late 19th century that dreams were considered a possible tool for clinical treatment and a subject worthy of scientific inquiry.

THE ADVENT OF PSYCHOANALYSIS

Sigmund Freud (1856–1939) started his career as a neurologist. Intrigued by the use of hypnosis in treating certain neurotic conditions, he turned his attention to the experiences of the **psyche**. The behavior of hypnotized subjects taught him that the patient was often unaware of the true motivations for his or her symptoms or behavior. Freud came to understand that the unconscious parts of the personality were powerful, hidden forces, often in conflict with each other. Thus, mind (spirit, soul) had a new dimension, previously unaddressed by physicians and philosophers. Dreams and dream analysis took on major significance in the new treatment, which he called psychoanalysis. Unconscious thoughts and impulses—usually frightening, dangerous, and unacceptable to society—could surface while the patient was asleep, while the forces keeping those ideas submerged relaxed their vigilance. By analyzing dreams, the therapist could help the patient achieve insight into the real meaning of his or her troublesome behavior. According to psychoanalytic theory, dreams provided access to the unconscious mind and were an expression of hidden, unfulfilled wishes.

EXPERIMENTAL PSYCHOLOGY AND BEHAVIORISM

During the early 20th century, another school of thought that was strongly critical of Freud's **mentalistic** theory of psychoanalysis took hold. The new science of **experimental psychology**, pioneered in the laboratory of Professor Wilhelm Wundt (1832–1920) in Leipzig, Germany, confined itself to the analysis of sensory experience, physiological processes, learning, and memory. Experimental psychology was the study of the "mind"—dreams were not considered appropriate for investigation.

The Russian physiologist Ivan Pavlov (1849–1936) had shown that dogs could be made to salivate at the sound of a tone by repeatedly pairing the tone with food. Salivation is an unlearned response to food but becomes conditioned to the new sound stimulus. Later, with the advent of behaviorism, a discipline pioneered by John Watson (1878–1958), psychology was limited to the study of observable and measurable behavior. Watson, who was trained as an experimental psychologist, worked with animals and spent his early career teaching at the University of Chicago. As a professor at Johns Hopkins University in Baltimore, Watson redefined psychology from the point of view of a behaviorist. Dreams, being totally subjective and not measurable, were regarded merely as mental aberrations of no real significance.

The advent of behaviorism in American psychology heralded a preoccupation with reducing behavior to stimulus and response connections that were anchored firmly in the nervous system. Watson demonstrated that emotions such as fear could be conditioned in the same way. In a 1920 study by Watson and his research assistant Rosalie Raynor, a young child was made to fear a white rat and other white furry objects by scaring him while he was playing with the rat. Later in the 20th century, American psychologist B. F. Skinner (1904–1990) demonstrated how events immediately following a behavior (reinforcement) facilitated the learning of that behavior. Skinner went on to become a psychology professor at Harvard and the most influential psychologist of his day. Using laboratory rats as his subjects, he devised methods of automatically recording bar-pressing behavior in rats to study the manner in which food reinforcements determine the learning and maintenance of that behavior. These principles were applied in many practical ways, such as teaching appropriate social behaviors to psychiatric patients, using **token economies** or developing teaching programs for children using behavior rewards and step-by-step learning. One program taught children cursive writing. Another was designed to teach psychology to college students. *Walden Two*, a novel Skinner wrote, described an ideal society fashioned entirely upon behavioral principles. Behaviorism redefined psychology, not as the study of "mind," but as a study of behavior.

BEHAVIORISM MODIFIED

By the end of the 20th century, psychologists realized that strict behaviorism left an important factor out of the equation: It ignored the importance of subjective mental events such as thoughts. Humans are more complex than the animals whose behavior during learning experiments led to the major principles of behaviorism. To many psychologists of the late 20th century, the approaches of Watson and Skinner seemed too mechanical. They ignored subjective reactions such as thoughts, feelings, and memories that may be irrelevant in animals but that clearly influence human behavior. People evaluate their situation and tell themselves certain things that help shape their emotions and behavior. In order to consider internal, subjective events (such as thoughts [**cognitions**] and feelings, as well as external rewards or punishments) in predicting behavior, a new approach was developed. Behavior therapy became cognitive behavior therapy.

Psychoanalytic thinking and the study of dreams again became acceptable to some psychologists. The development of computer technology also influenced how psychologists understood human thinking and learning. The logical and sequential steps of computer programs were considered models for human thinking. Psychologists today are less willing to accept dream content as solely representative of unconscious impulses than they were 100 years ago. Rather, the ideas of dreams are seen as representing perceptions, emotions, and memories that somehow get transformed into visual images, language, and feelings. This change coincides with the growing popularity of cognitive psychology that began in the 1970s and 1980s. Other psychologists continued to ignore dreams as inconsequential. As an area of focus, dreams are more appealing to psychologists who treat emotional problems than to those who adhere to rigorous research methodology.

So it was that ideas of the ancients and classical philosophers were discarded and reinvented in new forms. Today, behavioral **geneticists** recognize the value of learning the interactions between behavior and genetics. They seek, and sometimes find, genetic determinants of many human behaviors. Many clinical disorders, such as autism, depression, and schizophrenia, were understood to be not solely learned behavior but also to be genetically determined.

NATIVE AMERICAN RITUALS

Science may not be the only path to psychological insight. Native American beliefs and rituals have survived for centuries. In Native American culture, dreams and visions play a central role in understanding man's place in the universe (see Figure 5.1 and "Dream Catchers" box). They are a central part of the search for spiritual knowledge. Dreams are not distinguished from waking visions, both of which are understood to be sacred.

Among the native peoples of the Great Plains of North America, dreams and visions are used to explain waking experiences. The dream was not sharply distinguished from normal waking experience but was viewed as an altered state of awareness, important in achieving human potential. Each generation actively engages in "**vision quests**," in which a tribe member goes off alone to a special place and engages in rituals, such as the use of dream-enhancing materials. During these altered states of consciousness, Native Americans believe that they communicate with dream spirits. Awareness of space and time is altered.

The dreamer may cover great distances and move through the yearly seasonal cycle. He or she receives guidance and inspiration from the dream spirits in all aspects of life and returns with much knowledge and power. Both men and women engage in visionary experiences, often accompanied by pipe smoking, fasting, and praying. According to Native American beliefs, the dreamer is transported by the spirits to another world. In the dream he or she may receive instructions, often in symbolic form. Upon returning from a vision quest, the dreamer must

Figure 5.1 Dream catchers, such as the one held by this Yurok woman, are made by many Native American artists. The dream catcher is intended to filter out bad dreams and allow only good dreams to enter the mind.

await the time to use the newly acquired knowledge and power. Only mature individuals are thought to be capable of interpreting their experience. Meanings are not immediately apparent. The dreamer may share the visions with interpreters in secret dreaming societies. Dreams are rarely discussed verbally but may be revealed through special languages and dances. In this way, dreams are added to the tribal culture. They are integrated into tribal legends, rituals, and religious beliefs.

MAGIC, DREAMS, AND LITERATURE

For centuries, the task of analyzing dreams was relegated to professionals presumed to have the ability to access the mysterious or the magical. Seers, magicians, witch doctors, shamans, and prophets provided the guidance. Today, psychotherapists play this role. Do dreams have mystical meanings? Our legends and fables appear to accept the reality of magic. They depict accounts of magicians such as Gandalf and Merlin, who appear at significant points in the tale and effect dramatic interventions. The appearance of the obelisk in Arthur Clark's novel *2001: A Space Odyssey* precedes each significant level of progress in the evolution of humans. The movie *E.T.: The Extra-Terrestrial* awakens our hope that we are not alone in the universe. So it is not sur-

Dream Catchers

Although dream catchers are made by Native American artists from many nations, they are thought to have originated with the Ojibwe (also called the Chippewa) nation, whose homelands were around the Great Lakes. Ojibwe mothers took up the practice of weaving spider-like webs, thought to be magic, by using willow hoops and winding them with cordage from plants. They were made in the shape of a circle to represent the way the sun travels across the sky. The dream catcher is intended to filter out bad dreams and allow only good dreams to enter babies' minds. A small hole in the center of each dream catcher allows only the good dreams to come through. Dreams were destroyed by sunlight in the morning. It was traditional to place a feather in the center of the dream catcher. The baby would be entertained by watching the air move the feather and would learn the value of fresh air. Feathers of the owl were thought to impart wisdom; feathers of the eagle instilled courage. Dream catchers for children were not meant to last. Eventually, the willow dries out and the dream catcher collapses. This is meant to signify that childhood is temporary. Adult dream catchers use woven fiber to catch adult dreams. Today, dream catchers are still in use, not only by Native American people, but others as well. Many people who use a dream catcher believe it helps them sleep better.

prising that people tend to accept magical or mystical meaning in dreams and accept the pronouncements of the "experts" who interpret them.

Dreams play a prominent role in many movies, plays, literature, and poetry. The poet Samuel Taylor Coleridge (1772–1834) is said to have composed his poem "Kubla Khan" in a dream. The psychoanalyst Carl Jung (1875–1961) believed that we inherit a "collective unconscious" of memories filled with symbols reflecting the experience of previous generations (Figure 5.2). These symbols, called "**archetypes**," appear repeatedly in our dreams. Molecular biologists may eventually find evidence of inherited memories in our **DNA**. Jung's theories are discussed further in Chapter 6.

Jung believed that dream images are inherited and that they reflect universal primitive experiences that provide the material for our dreams and appear repeatedly in myths, legends, and folk tales. Such images pass on from generation to generation, not by training or experience, but because they are programmed into our brains at birth. Jungian analysts interpret dreams as representing universal archetypes such as magic, the hero, God, power, the wise old man, and death. The wise old man may be a physician, priest, healer, teacher, or magician. Who was the wise old man in *The Lord of the Rings*? Fairy tales such as *Red Riding Hood, Goldilocks, Cinderella,* and *Sleeping Beauty* are filled with such images.

> *"Hold your tongue!" said the Queen, turning purple.*
>
> *"I won't!" said Alice.*
>
> *"Off with her head!" The Queen shouted at the top of her voice. Nobody moved.*
>
> *"Who cares for you?" said Alice. She had grown to her full size by this time. "You're nothing but a pack of cards!"*

Figure 5.2 Carl Jung (1875–1961) is known as the founder of analytical psychology. He believed that we inherit a "collective unconscious" of memories filled with symbols reflecting the experience of previous generations.

At this the whole pack rose up into the air, and came flying down upon her; she gave a little scream, half of fright and half anger, and tried to beat them off, and found herself lying on the bank, with her head in the lap of her sister, who was gently brushing off some dead leaves that had fluttered down from the trees on her face.

"Wake up, Alice dear!" said her sister. "Why what a long sleep you've had!" . . .

So Alice got up and ran off, thinking while she ran, as well she might, what a wonderful dream it had been.

—Lewis Carroll
Alice's Adventures in Wonderland, 1865

How realistic are Alice's adventures, interpreted as a dream? The same question applies to Dorothy's visit to the Land of Oz. In the movie *The Wizard of Oz*, Dorothy's Oz, shown in color, is a lot more interesting than her real home in Kansas, shown in black and white. Alice's rabbit hole is Dorothy's yellow brick road. Such tales, like dreams, are intriguing to children because they provide entrance to the world of fantasy, where the reader or viewer is encouraged to suspend reality and indulge in make-believe. Do they appeal because they arouse infantile and familiar wishes and fears that are there all along, already programmed into our memories? Does Wonderland's Duchess, feeding her boy in a pepper-filled kitchen, arouse ambivalent feelings that children already feel toward their own mothers? "*Speak harshly to your little boy. And beat him when he sneezes. He only does it to annoy, because he knows it teases.*"

We embrace the myths embedded in our literature and art perhaps because we need to believe in some greater universal entity. We crave the supernatural, some extraterrestrial force, to explain the confusion in our lives. The mystical, the magical —the **metaphysical**—has universal appeal. However, scientists have taught us to be skeptical of wondrous and magical explanations. They have shown repeatedly that the simplest explanations are often the most reasonable. This principle, known as Ockham's razor, is attributed to the medieval philosopher William of Ockham (1285–1349). It states that one should not increase, beyond what is necessary, the number of explanations for anything. One should "shave off" extra concepts and assumptions. This principle is the basis of scientific theory building. Scientists seek cause-and-effect relationships to explain natural events. Until it is shown that natural processes and mechanisms cannot explain human experience and behavior, they should not be abandoned. So it is with dreams.

Dreams do contain images that may represent something different from how they appear in the dream. We discuss how this happens in Chapter 7. Sometimes, the images mean the same thing to other dreamers as well, since they share similar cultural or family experiences. Often, they represent only your own unique meanings because your personality is unique. There is no shortcut to understanding dreams. Nevertheless, with perseverance and an understanding of the dream process, one can learn to interpret dreams. Dreams can sometimes help you address issues, worries, and concerns that you would not ordinarily consider because dreams are so fleeting and you are more preoccupied with everyday problems. This book attempts to integrate a variety of informational sources and to present a commonsense approach to understanding and interpreting dreams. It is not the final word, but it should help you formulate your own opinion. Perhaps it can provide a springboard to new insights and personal growth.

■ **Learn more about the ways people try to understand dreams**
Search the Internet for *dream analysis* and *dream archetypes*.

Theories of Dreams and Application in Psychotherapy

Dreams are often most profound when they seem most crazy.

—Sigmund Freud, 1908

It is 1879. You are Ludwig, a doctoral student at the University of Leipzig Psychological Laboratory. Professor Wilhelm Wundt, the director of the laboratory, is asking you to observe an apple and describe your sensations. Such studies reveal the true nature of conscious experience.

"Professor Wundt, may I tell you about a dream I had last night? I would like to do an investigation of this phenomenon of dreams."

"Verboten!" (Forbidden)

"Professor, surely no human experience should be ignored."

"Dumkoff! (Dumbbell) Dreams are nonsense. In sleep there are no sensations. They are not worthy of investigation. You are no longer welcome in my laboratory. Go do your dreaming somewhere else."

*   *   *

I am 10 years old and have been taken to see Dr. John Watson, a behaviorist, at the Johns Hopkins Psychology Clinic in Baltimore. It is 1925. I am afraid of dogs. I dream about dogs every night—they are scary dreams. A giant bulldog is chasing me, and I am running away. Just as he is about to jump, I scream, but nothing comes out. I wake up. The bulldog reminds me of my father, but Dr. Watson doesn't seem interested in that. He is going to bring a dog into the room with me while I am eating. All I know is I don't want to be here.

* * *

It is Vienna in 1915. You are Katrina, a patient of the young neurologist Sigmund Freud, now the rage of the city. He has developed a bold, new theory about neuroses. You have come to him because of a strange malady. You have lost control of your leg muscles. Your doctor insists there is nothing wrong with your legs, yet you cannot walk. You are asked by Dr. Freud to reveal the dream you had last night.

"I am in a field. There is a magnificent, wild stallion. I know I should stay away because he is dangerous, but I am drawn to the animal. Just as I am about to pet it, the horse is transformed into a giant, green snake. I am repulsed by it. It jumps on me. I scream and wake up."

The doctor asks you to let your mind wander and bring to mind what the images in your dream remind you of. He interprets your thoughts in ways that are embarrassing—improper thoughts for a young, unmarried woman to have these days. He says your dreams reveal unconscious sexual motivations. It is difficult for you to accept such outrageous explanations. And yet . . . curiously, your legs feel stronger.

* * *

I am Rasheen, top of my senior class, star running back, and, in my daydreams, in love with Jennifer Lopez. Yet, I feel depressed all the time. No matter how well I do, I always feel that I should have done better. I have a dream in which I am a world-class track star.

I am doing the pole vault in an important meet. After each jump, the bar is raised and, each time I succeed, but I must keep jumping. There is no end. J. Lo is in the stands examining my report card. She is writing me a recommendation for college, but her pen is out of ink. I am seeing Dr. Kind, a cognitive psychologist at the community mental health clinic. He says I am depressed because I tell myself irrational thoughts.

PSYCHOANALYTIC THEORY

No other figure in history has had as great an influence on contemporary psychology as Sigmund Freud. Freud's influence was not only on psychology but on Western culture as well. "Psychoanalysis," the therapeutic technique developed by Freud in the late 19th and early 20th centuries, is a household word, as are many of the concepts deriving from his theories of personality, development, and the psychoneuroses (e.g., oral personality, anal personality, superego, libido, Freudian slip).

It is impossible to fully appreciate Freud's understanding of dreams without some theoretical background. Prior to Freud, human personality and motivation were viewed as purely conscious and mostly rational. The prevailing psychology in the 1920s and 1930s, when Freud reached his peak of popularity, was **trait theory**. Behaviors were explained as the result of traits, habits, and values such as honesty, industriousness, ambition, and sentimentality. **Traits** were defined as long-lasting predispositions to act and feel in certain ways. Traits provided the energy and direction for behavior. They were measured by self-ratings, ratings by others, and personal documents, such as letters and diaries. They include measures of attitudes, motives, and values. After Freud, behavior was no longer considered entirely conscious or always rational.

Freud's use of hypnosis in treatment led him to appreciate the existence of a vast and powerful unconscious part of the personality—a motivating force that determined behavior but operated outside of conscious awareness. Later, Freud differentiated three major parts of the personality:

- Ego: The conscious part of personality that interacts with the outside world.
- Superego: The part of personality that includes the ideal for which we strive and the conscience that punishes the ego for transgressions.
- Id: The unconscious seat of instincts such as aggression and sex drive (see "The Unconscious" box).

Freud saw sexual motives as the cause of all neuroses. The three parts of personality, Freud believed, were in constant conflict with each other. This formulation of personality was purely theoretical. It was Freud's attempt to account for the behavior, symptoms, and associations of his patients. The id strives for expression of instinctual drives. The superego is motivated toward control of the instincts and socially acceptable behavior. The ego mediates between the two—trying to satisfy the demands of a cruel and punishing superego by the use of **defense mechanisms** such as **repression** to keep unacceptable thoughts, memories, and ideas within the unconscious. A vigilant "**censor**," part of the ego, served as the gatekeeper, preventing unacceptable or threatening thoughts from entering consciousness (see "Dream Censorship" box). Sometimes, the ego found ways to allow instinctual expression in socially acceptable ways. Sports, for example, are an acceptable way of expressing aggression.

During sleep, the censor relaxes its vigilance. Nevertheless, the true meaning of dream images is disguised, which accounts for the bizarre nature of dreams. According to Freud, slips of the tongue ("Freudian slips") are another source of a person's real intent. Freud initially used hypnosis to access the unconscious but abandoned the technique when he felt the results were only temporary. He developed a method of free association instead. In free association, the patient, reclining on a sofa and subjected to only minimal external stimulation, is asked to say whatever comes to mind, concealing no thought, however trivial or embarrassing it might seem.

The Unconscious

Where, and in what connection, is it supposed to have been proved that a man can possess knowledge without knowing that he does so, which is the assumption that we are making of the dreamer? . . .

The proof to which I refer was found in the sphere of hypnotic phenomena. In the year 1889, I was present at the remarkably impressive demonstrations by [Ambroise-Auguste] Liebeault [1823–1904] and [Hippolyte] Bernheim [1837–1919], in Nancy, and there I witnessed the following experiment. A man was placed in a condition of somnambulism [sleepwalking], and then made to go through all sorts of hallucinatory experiences. On being awakened, he seemed at first to know nothing at all of what had taken place during his hypnotic sleep. Bernheim then asked him in so many words to tell him what had happened while he was under hypnosis. The man replied that he could not remember anything. Bernheim, however, insisted upon it, pressed him, and assured him that he did know and that he must remember, and lo and behold! The man wavered, began to reflect, and remembered in a shadowy fashion first one of the occurrences which had been suggested to him, then something else, his recollection growing increasingly clear and complete until finally it was brought to light without a single gap. . . .
—Sigmund Freud, 1956

While writing a prescription for a woman who was especially weighted down by the financial burden of the treatment, I was interested to hear her say suddenly:

"Please do not give me *big bills,* because I cannot swallow them." Of course she meant to say *pills.*

—Sigmund Freud, *Psychopathology of Everyday Life*

Freud used dream analysis in conjunction with free association to detect hidden sources of conflict. The dream content itself served as a stimulus for associations to the various dream images. In analyzing his patients, as well as in conducting self-analysis of his own dreams throughout his life, Freud became convinced that dreams were a valid method for uncovering repressed thoughts and feelings, disguising the latent content.

Freud believed that dreams express unconscious wishes in disguised or symbolic form. The actual dream events were labeled the "**manifest content**," whereas the true meaning of the symbol was the "**latent content**." The methods of camouflage, disguising the latent content, included the use of symbols, metaphors, condensation of images, new words (**neologisms**) that combine two or more meanings, and displacement of one image by another. These mechanisms are explained more fully in Chapter 7.

Freud found that many common symbols occurred in the dreams of his patients, and that they represented the same thing. Kings and queens, for example, stood for one's parents. Nevertheless, Freud cautioned against the uncritical acceptance of universal symbols. Dreams must be interpreted in context, he cautioned, and only through the associations of each individual to the dream image. Not all dream images are meaningful. Often, images reflect experiences or perceptions, however inconsequential, formed during the day before the dream. Freud labeled this dream content the "**day residue**."

Freud's approach has been called "depth psychology." Freud believed that personality was like an onion, with many layers of meaning. No image had only one meaning; it could

Dream Censorship

In 1956, Freud reported that when patients were asked to "free associate" during treatment, they exhibited *resistance* in addressing certain topics or following certain trains of thought. He interpreted this resistance as a censorship by one part of the personality—a reluctance to admit ideas into consciousness that were threatening to the individual. This explanation is based upon the concept of a personality divided against itself, with a large part consisting of unconscious impulses. This same resistance was also found in dreams. So strong is this censorship that when the meaning is suggested to the individual, he or she may vigorously deny its validity. These ideas and impulses, often forbidden wishes, do manage to find expression in dreams, but they must be disguised. For this reason, the apparent meaning of the dream taken at face value (manifest content) must be interpreted to reveal its true meaning (latent content).

. . . the process of dream-work has nevertheless been operative to some extent, for the wish has been transformed into a reality and, usually, the thoughts also into visual images. Here no interpretation is necessary; we have only to retrace both these transformations. The further operations of the dream-work, as seen in the other types of (adult) dreams, we call dream-distortion, and here the original ideas have to be restored by our interpretive work.

—Sigmund Freud, 1956

Source: Freud, S. *A General Introduction to Psychoanalysis*. Garden City: Doubleday, 1956.

have multiple meanings at different levels of interpretation. Freud believed the personality to be similar to an iceberg in that the hidden portions, representing the unconscious, were—by far—the most extensive part. He considered himself a kind of archaeologist, digging deeper and deeper to uncover hidden meanings.

JUNGIAN THEORY

A colleague of Freud, Carl Jung, established his own school of analytic thought and therapy. Born in Switzerland, Jung studied medicine at the University of Basel and traveled to Zurich to work in a mental hospital. His work with schizophrenic patients led him to develop his theory of the **collective unconscious**. The fantasies and dreams of his disturbed patients, Jung believed, were similar to the myths of contemporary and ancient cultures. He felt that these themes were passed down in the structure of the brain and nervous system from generation to generation. These themes, called archetypes, were universal and exerted a strong influence upon behavior. Archetypes such as the self, God, and the magician appear through symbols in our dreams. Not every archetype is developed equally in every individual. They express themselves in the development of different types of individuals, such as those who are oriented toward other people or toward ideas and intellectual pursuits. Jung collaborated with Freud from 1907 to 1913. He broke with Freud because he could not accept Freud's belief that the sex instinct was the sole determinant of behavior.

GESTALT THEORY

Another approach to psychotherapy was developed by Fritz Perls in 1969. Perls (1893–1970) was born and educated in Berlin, Germany. He received a medical degree and specialized in psychiatry. After serving in the German Army as a medic in

World War I, he moved to Vienna and received psychoanalytic training. In 1946, he immigrated to the United States and abandoned psychoanalytic treatment, developing his own ideas which he labeled **gestalt therapy** (see "Perception and Gestalt" box). He established the New York Institute for Gestalt Therapy in 1952. Eventually, he settled in Big Sur, California, giving workshops and seminars at the Esalen Institute. He achieved an international reputation as an innovator in psychotherapy.

Perls believed that people must take responsibility for themselves—for what they are thinking, feeling, and doing—in the

Perception and Gestalt

Gestalt psychology was developed in Germany during the early part of the 20th century. The German word *gestalt* translates roughly as pattern or form. Gestalt psychology emphasizes the idea that the whole pattern of stimuli determines the manner in which the parts are perceived. Gestalt psychologists attempted to determine how the brain organizes our perceptions into meaningful wholes. One visual example is that an image contains both a "figure" and a "background." The figure appears to be more solid and to stand in front of the background. Figure and background may reverse from one moment to the next. In this illustration do you see a vase against a background or do you see the outlines of two faces? Can you reverse them?

present, which Perls believed to be more important than the past and the future. Gestalt therapy emphasizes the direct experiencing of feelings rather than merely talking about them. The approach to dreams is not merely to analyze them but to bring them to life. The patient is asked to relive the dream as if it were happening now. The dreamer in gestalt therapy lists all the characters, events, and moods of the dream. He or she is then asked to act out each of the roles, becoming each character and every object in turn. Each element in the dream is assumed in some way to be a projection of the dreamer. The technique allows the patient to recognize and address inconsistent and contradictory parts of his or her personality. The individual learns to integrate various parts of the personality and to appreciate the differences.

A woman receiving gestalt therapy reported the following dream in the present tense:

I have three monkeys in a cage—one big monkey and two little ones. I feel very attached to these monkeys, although they are creating a lot of chaos in a cage that is divided into three separate spaces. They are fighting with one another. The big monkey is fighting with the little monkey. They are getting out of the cage, and they are clinging onto me. I feel like pushing them away from me. I feel totally overwhelmed by the chaos that they are creating around me. I turn to my mother and tell her that I need help, that I can no longer handle these monkeys because they are driving me crazy. I feel very sad and very tired, and I feel discouraged. I am walking away from the cage thinking that I really love these monkeys, yet I will have to get rid of them. I am telling myself that I am like everyone else. I get pets, and then when things get rough I want to get rid of them. I am trying very hard to find a solution to keeping these monkeys and not allowing them to have such a terrific effect on me. Before I wake up from my dream, I am making the decision to put each monkey in a separate cage, and maybe that is the way to keep them.

The therapist asked the client to become each of the parts of her dream, each monkey as well as the cage. She realized that the dream expressed a conflict she was having with her husband and her two children. She recognized that she both loved and resented her family. She needed to have a dialogue with her family and express her conflicting feelings. The family needed to learn to communicate better and try to improve their relationships. No interpretation by the therapist was necessary for the woman to reach these conclusions.

COGNITIVE THEORY

While Freudian theory and treatment maintained its hold on popular thinking and was a significant influence on literature, art, movies, and the media, it lost its appeal to many scientists and practitioners. The theory was, in many instances, untestable. It offered an explanation for the presence of symptoms as well as their absence. It was based on 19th-century concepts of physical energy. The treatment was time-consuming and expensive—not available to most people of ordinary means. Furthermore, even Freud's disciples broke away from orthodox psychoanalysis and developed new approaches. Behaviorism took hold and presented more rapid methods with direct treatment of symptoms using the conditioning methods of Pavlov and Watson (see "Watson on Dreams" box). During the later part of the 20th century, however, there was a renewed interest among psychologists in **subjective events**—perceptions, thoughts, ideas, attitudes, values, and feelings. These could not be directly observed but might be inferred from the individual's verbal report. Even psychoanalysis became fashionable once again. Cognitive psychologists began to examine human behavior from a cognitive viewpoint. Rather than trying to account for responses solely on the basis of stimuli preceding those responses and rewards following them, they factored in the influence of intervening thoughts (cognitions). Some turned their attention, as Freud had, to dream analysis, examining associations to dream images, but without assumptions about a dynamic unconscious or a censor directing dream traffic. They accepted the premise that dreams are meaningful but believe that dreams primarily reflect waking life.

In 1996, American psychiatry professor Clara Hill of the University of Maryland developed a dream-formation theory and a method of dream interpretation. Her model derives from the the-

Watson on Dreams

John Watson was criticized for his assertion that most emotions are learned. With Rosalie Raynor in 1920, he conducted a study of "Little Albert," the 11-month-old son of a worker in the hospital at Johns Hopkins University. It remains today one of the most famous and controversial studies in the psychological literature.

Albert was taught to fear a white rat, an animal that originally evoked his interest. While Albert was playing with the animal, the investigators struck a steel bar with a hammer just behind Albert's head. The child was startled and, when the bar was struck a second time, he began to whimper. (This is not a procedure that would be permitted today.)

On several occasions after the first week, when Albert was brought back to the laboratory and shown the rat, he began to cry. Whimpering and withdrawal also occurred when Albert was shown other furry stimuli—a rabbit, a dog, a seal coat, cotton, wool, a Santa Claus mask, and even Watson's own hair, which was streaked with white. The same fear responses occurred to each of these objects. Watson explained that he had demonstrated how fears are learned at home. Albert was never brought back to the hospital to decondition him of his fear of furry objects. Later studies have shown that this would have been possible.

ories of Freud and Jung, as well as more recent cognitive theories of brain function. Hill argues that dreams are triggered by events in waking life and are an attempt to integrate waking experiences into existing memory structures (past thoughts, feelings, and actions). They are unique to the individual. The dreamer tells him- or herself a story during the dream, connecting present events and past memories. This formulation assumes that dreams represent waking rather than unconscious conflicts. The dreamer tries to understand present experiences in light of past memories. When current events are too painful or different from past memories, the dream does not work and the individual may remain troubled or suffer from recurrent dreams and nightmares.

DREAMS AND PSYCHOTHERAPY

Learn from your dreams what you lack.

—W. H. Auden, British poet, 1907–1973

Psychotherapy involves two or more people allied with a common goal (Figure 6.1). The relationship between therapist and patient is a significant part of the treatment process. The patient often projects onto the therapist roles and characteristics that go beyond their actual interaction. Patients may act out personality conflicts in therapy, reenacting real-life situations. At times, the therapist may represent father, mother, or other significant persons.

Psychotherapists operate from the framework of various theories and use markedly different treatment strategies. They attempt to assist their patients with problems of adjustment to the demands of daily living. They address feelings of happiness, anxiety, depression, or anger. They work with problems of eating, shyness, anger, or self-esteem.

Therapists who use dream analysis believe it can help in every phase of the treatment process. Many therapists use an

Figure 6.1 A teenage girl undergoes psychotherapy.

approach to dream analysis that is similar to what we present in the appendix of this book. They ask you to trace your associations to the dream, and they guide you in searching for meaning. Therapists will not, however, make interpretations for you. They may challenge your meanings and suggest some new directions. They enter your subjective world but maintain a respectful distance. Once you arrive at a meaning that feels right to you, they may suggest an action plan to make the most productive use of your new understanding. The therapist probes for possible meanings to specific dream images, and also for the emotions experienced during the dream or in the retelling of it, as well as the dream ending. They may challenge you to create a more satisfying ending. During the discovery phase of dream analysis, the therapist avoids making interpretations or giving advice. During the insight phase, the therapist plays the role of facilitator, rather than learned professor.

THE CASE OF DORA

The first published case of dream analysis occurred over 100 years ago. The case of Dora, published by Sigmund Freud in 1902, was titled "Analysis of a Case of **Hysteria.**" In the late 18th and early 19th centuries, hypnosis was used to treat certain conditions presumed to have a psychological origin (that is, no physical cause could be found). Freud, trained to use hypnosis with such patients, later abandoned the technique in favor of his own "psychoanalytic" methods of free association and dream analysis.

Vienna in the early 1900s was a Victorian society where sexual matters were not discussed, especially not with or among young ladies of proper upbringing. Freud discarded that prohibition. While his theories and methods are not universally accepted (and were not at the time), they provide the flavor of the dream interpretation that was characteristic of early psychoanalysis.

Dora was a 17-year-old girl living with her father, mother, and younger brother in Vienna. She was referred to Dr. Freud after a several-year history of a nervous cough and migraine headaches. More recently, she seemed chronically tired and could not concentrate. She was not getting along well with her parents. She avoided social contact and had a fear of men. She reported a vague pressure in the upper part of her body. One day, after an argument with her father, she lost consciousness. This was the incident that resulted in the referral to Freud. The doctor's immediate impression was that Dora's symptoms were hysterical, the result of some mental trauma and a disturbance in sexuality.

Dora's family was wealthy. Her father, who owned a factory, had recently recovered from a serious illness. During this time, the family became friendly with another couple, Mr. and Mrs. K. Mrs. K had nursed Dora's father during his illness, and he was very grateful to her. Mrs. K was very kind to Dora and sometimes gave her expensive gifts. Sometimes Dora stayed at their home. Dora related a dream to Freud. She had experienced the same dream four times:

A house was on fire. My father was standing beside my bed and woke me up. I dressed myself quickly. Mother wanted to stop and save her jewel case, but father said: "I will not let myself and my two children be burnt for the sake of your jewel case." We hurried downstairs and as soon as I was outside, I woke up.

When questioned about the dream, Dora reported, "Father was having a dispute with mother in the last few days, because she locks the dining room at night. My brother's room, you see, has no separate entrance, but can only be reached through the dining room. Father does not want my brother to be locked in like that at night. He says it will not do; something might happen in the night so that it might be necessary to leave the room."

Dora associated the figure of her father in the dream with an earlier incident, when she had been staying with Mr. and Mrs. K. She awakened one night to find Mr. K standing over her bed. The next night, she found a key and locked her room, but soon after, the key was missing. She believed that Mr. K had taken it and feared that Mr. K would again come into her room. She dressed herself quickly each morning. After several days, she demanded that her father take her home. Dora also recalled an earlier incident at age 14 when Mr. K had kissed her, leaving Dora with a feeling of disgust.

Freud saw a connection between Dora's statements that she woke up once she got out of the house in her dream. This was an expression of her thought that she would get no sleep until she is out of the house. Another important element in the dream was the jewel case. Dora related an incident in which her father had given her mother an expensive bracelet. Her mother had wanted something different and in anger told her husband to give it to someone else. Dora, who overheard the argument, and craved her father's attention, would have accepted the bracelet with pleasure. Freud explained the dream to Dora in this way:

> . . . The meaning of the dream is now becoming clearer. You said to yourself, "This man (Mr. K) is persecuting me; he wants to force his way into my room. . . . if anything happens, it will be Father's fault. . . ." For that reason, in the dream, you chose a situation that expresses the opposite—a danger from which your father is saving you.

Freud believed that dreams express infantile wishes. In this case, Dora had strong feelings for her father and wanted to give him the love her mother withheld. The wish for her father was even more threatening to Dora than her fear of Mr. K and had to be kept unconscious.

Dora was able to confront both Mr. and Mrs. K. Mr. K admitted his misconduct. Mrs. K admitted to having an affair with Dora's father. Dora was vindicated. Her family severed relations with the Ks. Dora's symptoms disappeared. She was later able to give up her infantile wishes for her father and to marry.

■ **Learn more about dreams and psychotherapy** Search the Internet for *Sigmund Freud, Carl Jung*, and *gestalt therapy*.

7 The Work of Dreams

The soul in sleep gives proof of its divine nature.

—Cicero, Greek poet (106–43 B.C.)

I can never decide whether my dreams are the result of my thoughts or my thoughts are the result of my dreams.

—D. H. Lawrence, English novelist (1885–1930)

DO DREAMS HAVE MEANING?

Therapists who use dreams in treatment assume that the dreams have meaning. This assumption is based on clinical experience. The content of the dream, the client's associations, and his or her life experiences, including everyday concerns and problems, must form a consistent and cohesive pattern. Often, clients will grasp onto an interpretation on their own and report a feeling of recognition or new awareness (**insight**). One significant part of dream content was labeled the "day residue" by Freud. Events experienced during the day, no matter how insignificant they seemed at the time, can provide the nucleus of the dream. Thoughts entertained during the day may also contribute to dream formation, especially if they are important to the individual or are emotionally charged.

The content of a dream may be a major distortion of some underlying thought. We will examine how these distortions occur shortly. Although the distortion is enough to disguise the true meaning of the dream, it is not so far removed from reality that it cannot be unraveled. The visual image or dream sequence bears some relationship to the object or person it represents. Sometimes, the similarity is transparent: This is the case when the images have a prior association with the true meaning they represent. The association may exist through words that sound different but are similar in meaning (synonyms), or words that sound the same but mean different things (homonyms). The connection may be a slang usage. It may be a creative play on words. The connection may simply be through things that have occurred together. A swimming pool in a dream may result from associated images of swimming, water, parties, July 4th, swimming lessons, bathing suits. Images may become increasingly removed from the real meaning because of such associations. Dreams often seem to have multiple meanings that are intertwined. A relationship with a friend or family member may be depicted. The dream seems to be a reworking of an actual event. Yet, on another level, it may be clear that the person in the dream really represents someone else. If this is so, an entirely different meaning is implied. Freud said dreams were "**overdetermined.**" Some therapists believe that every character in the dream, on some level, is really the dreamer. Dreams may be a replay of past events that turned out poorly. Perhaps the dream provides a better ending. The dream may also portray an anticipated future event. We will examine how these distortions occur shortly and suggest how dreams may be formed.

Dreams include feelings. You can have dreams that leave you feeling happy, sad, or angry. You may feel embarrassment. Sometimes, the emotion in the dream appears inappropriate to what was being depicted. The emotion may be a clue to what the story really meant.

Dreams involve sensations—you see things; you hear what you or other people say; you may even experience touch, smells, and tastes.

Dreams can be illogical or silly. In a dream, you may devise a brilliant solution to a problem, only to wake up be unable to see or remember the logic of your brilliant solution. One source of this problem may be that dreams compress time. The time sequence in a dream is completely unrealistic. To the dreamer, it appears quite natural. A dream that seems to last for hours may actually take place in only a few seconds of real time.

Dreams tell a story. There is a sequence of events. Things happen. Some dreamers experience a story that unfolds over two or more separate dreams. Other dreamers repeat the same dream over and over. When two dreams appear in sequence, the second dream sometimes provides clues to the first.

Dream content can be classified on the basis of theme or meaning. The author kept a running account of his dreams for 18 months. While there were hundreds of dreams with different content, once interpreted, the same dozen or so themes tended to recur.

Calvin Hall (1909–1985), one of the most creative psychologists of his day, made significant contributions to the study of personality and behavior genetics. During much of his career, he was professor and chairman of the Psychology Department of Case Western Reserve University. Later, he switched his research interest to the study of dreams over time. He collected more than 50,000 dream reports. Hall developed a cognitive theory of dreams, which he believed used metaphors to express the dreamer's concepts of self, family, friends, and the social environment. He found a high consistency in themes that occurred in the same individual, even in individuals who had undergone

radical life changes. Their dreams included conflicts over relationships, freedom versus security, moral issues, sex roles, and
life and death.

Dreams express feelings, solve problems, and reveal wishes or
needs. Recurring dreams probably represent our most pressing
motives or unresolved issues. Some believe that until those
problems are resolved, the events cannot be stored into long-
term memory.

DREAM PROCESSES

Dreams feature strange things. The images we experience in
dreams have been described as condensation, neologisms, displacement, symbols, and metaphors. Some psychologists who
study dreams believe that such mechanisms are purposeful,
unconscious attempts to disguise the real meaning of a dream
(repressed, socially unacceptable impulses), yet we can invoke
simpler explanations based on associations of which we may
be unaware.

Condensation

Condensation refers to the process in which two or more ideas or
concepts are merged into a composite image that expresses both
meanings. For example, the features of two or more people may
be combined in one person. Freud believed that the entire dream
occurs in a very condensed form. A dream may take the space of
a brief paragraph. The analyst interpreting the meaning of that
paragraph may require several pages of writing or even an entire
chapter in a book. A man dreams that he is watching someone
struggling to hold a cylindrical balloon on ropes. The dreamer's
son-in-law had done just that in the Thanksgiving Day parade in
New York City. The dream appeared to relate to conflicts the
dreamer knew his son-in law was having and his struggle to maintain control. Yet, the dreamer himself feels pulled in several direc-

tions in real life, sometimes by his son-in-law. Thus, the dream condensed two ideas of control into a single image.

Neologisms

One type of condensation is where a made-up word, or **neologism**, is coined to combine two ideas. An 18-year-old girl dreamed that she was riding an "expressolater" to a date with her boyfriend. The word in her dream referred to a very rapid escalator. She was looking forward to the date and wanted the time to pass quickly. She frequently met her date for coffee. The neologism also combined the image of espresso at the coffeehouse.

Displacement

Displacement is the process by which the meaning associated with one object or person is attached to something or someone else. The real object or person does not appear in the dream. A man dreamed of being at a vacation resort with a female coworker. In the dream, the man felt guilty for not being at work. The coworker really represented the man's wife, who had chided him for spending all his time working rather than saving time for fun. There was also guilt at being with an attractive coworker and not his wife. In reality, the dreamer and coworker were working on a time-sensitive job. The coworker in the dream represented herself but was also a displacement of feelings the dreamer harbored involving his wife. The dream had contradictory meanings—guilt over working and guilt over not working. Dreams may not seem to make sense, yet, in this case, it was not illogical because **conflict** was involved.

Symbols

Symbols are dream images that express a meaning larger than what the symbol itself literally represents. We use symbols almost constantly in life. Shorthand is a system of symbols for longer words or sentences. Logos are symbols that come to represent a product—the Nike "swoosh" or the interlocking rings for the Olympics are two examples. Traffic signs and computer icons are also symbols. The symbol may or may not look like the object it represents. The symbol has been associated in some way with the object, but the connection may not be obvious. Freud cautioned against the acceptance of universal symbols but listed many symbols that mean the same thing to people who grow up in the same culture. Some analysts interpret dreams of falling as expressions of anxiety about overreaching one's abilities in personal or professional life. Advertising makes ample use of symbols of sexuality, success, and achievement to sell products (see "Sexual Symbols" box).

Dreams of fire have been interpreted as symbolic of strong emotions such as love and anger. Dreams of being chased may represent feelings of persecution. Dreams of nakedness suggest a sense of shame. The dreamer's associations to the image are more significant than the image itself.

Metaphors

Metaphors in dreams are a type of symbol that appear to be a clever literary product. Metaphors appear in everyday speech, literature, and poetry. Dream metaphors are based on word associations, not the work of an English teacher in our unconscious. A woman was planning to change her insurance carrier. She dreamed of changing trains at a subway station. A train is a carrier. Why did she associate a subway train, rather than a bus, or taxi, or truck, or porter? One would need to know her associations to the word *carrier*. The woman had recently visited Paris, where the subway is called the Metro. Her insurance carrier was Metropolitan Life.

A teenage boy dreamed of a policewoman wielding a large battleaxe, getting ready to destroy a case of beer. He associated the term *battleaxe* with a popular (at the time) slang expression used to refer to a forceful, domineering, unattractive woman. The policewoman in the dream represented one of his teachers, whom he said was always "on his case."

The subway train, battleaxe, and case of beer are all examples of metaphors.

Not every image in our dreams reveals an important personality issue. Sometimes, dream images are not symbols at all, and simply represent what they appear to represent. Sometimes, images are just "noise" in the system.

We can now answer two important questions that we have already touched upon. The mechanisms outlined above, which serve to disguise and distort dreams, suggest that dreams do have meaning—in the sense that they refer to something real;

Sexual Symbols

While Freud argued against the universal meaning of symbols, he was inconsistent about this point. The number of things represented symbolically, he said, was limited and included the human body, parents, children, brothers and sisters, birth, death, and nakedness. Certain symbols, he found, occurred so frequently that they did convey a similar meaning to different people. Male sexual organs, for example, were often represented by both males and females as objects such as sticks, umbrellas, poles, and trees.

Female sexual organs were often represented as things that have the property of enclosing a space or acting as a receptacle: caves, boxes, doors, and gates. Breasts appear as apples, peaches, or other fruits.

Source: Freud, S. *A General Introduction to Psychoanalysis*. Garden City: Doubleday, 1956.

that there is an underlying need, memory, or experience that is being expressed; and that the dream is of significance to the life of the dreamer.

DO DREAMS HAVE PURPOSE?

The issue of whether dreams have purpose is more complicated. There is little evidence to support the contention that dreams represent the surfacing of forbidden, unconscious impulses that are kept submerged by an equally unconscious censor serving a harsh and unforgiving superego. Can dream content represent motives, needs, and wishes that are not typically a part of everyday conscious awareness? We have already stated that this is, indeed, the case. Can dreams have another purpose? They can in a physiological sense, such as processing information or "downloading" it to permanent memory, as has been suggested by some theorists and described in Chapter 2. We can conclude that dreams have meaning, possibly a physiological purpose, but likely not a psychological purpose.

HOW DREAMS ARE FORMED

The process of forming a dream seems to require a great deal of creativity and effort. All the metaphors and symbols that appear in dreams suggest that something or someone is directing the process. If it were a movie, it would require a director, a producer, writers, set designers, makeup artists, music directors, an orchestra, and actors. Psychoanalytic theory suggests that there are three directors (id, ego, and superego) within us that dictate our behavior and are in conflict with each other. A map of the areas of the brain's motor cortex, which controls body movements, looks like a little man ("homunculus"), but body movements are not dreams. The more reasonable view is that the sleeping brain processes limited information from the visual cortex, limbic system, and other areas, and integrates it with memories and associations.

The following hypothetical example illustrates how symbols and metaphors might enter into dream formation:

> Jacqui is flunking history. She's tried hard but has been under a great deal of pressure at home. She works after school in a bakery to bring home some extra money. She finds history boring. She fell behind in her reading assignments and flunked a major exam. When a term paper was assigned, she felt overwhelmed. A friend of hers, knowing her dilemma, offered her an old term paper, written for a different teacher. A good grade on the paper might help her get a passing grade in the class. There was little chance of getting caught. She handed in the friend's paper as her own, but immediately felt guilty about it. Jacqui received a grade of 75. She was thinking of confessing to the teacher and offering to write her own paper. It was this problem with which Jacqui was wrestling when she fell asleep.

Let's assume that the words *term paper* were rattling around in Jacqui's brain. These words activated other thoughts of notepads, ballpoint pens, hard work, encyclopedias, grades, and staying up late. These associations led to others: paper towels, stationery, paper clips, paper airplanes, newspaper, comic strips, current events, reporters, and newsstands. Nerve impulses produce images and emotions. She dreams. It is not difficult to interpret her dream:

> I am walking to the corner newsstand. I am buying a newspaper. The man asks for $75. I look in my purse and it is empty. I tell the man I will return tomorrow with the money. The vendor takes back the paper from me. I plead with him. I must have the paper back. He refuses to give it to me. I pull the paper from his hands and run. I look down. The paper is now a magazine. The cover says *True Confessions*. I feel guilty.

In this chapter, we looked at the process by which dreams are formed and the various mechanisms that disguise the meanings of the dream images—the associations, memories, metaphors, symbols, and a sleeping brain that tends to jumble things up a bit.

■ **Learn more about the purpose of dreams** Search the Internet for *dream function* and *dream formation.*

8 | Sleep and Dreaming in Your Life

Once I, Chuang Tzu, dreamed that I was a butterfly, a butterfly flying about, feeling that I was enjoying myself. It did not know that it was Chuang. Suddenly, I awoke and was myself again, the veritable Chuang. I do not know whether it was then Chuang dreaming that he was a butterfly or whether I am now a butterfly dreaming that it is Chuang. But between Chuang and a butterfly there must be a difference.

—Chuang Tzu, Chinese philosopher, 300 B.C.

As I live and am a man, this is an unexaggerated tale—my dreams become the substance of my life.

—Samuel Taylor Coleridge, British poet, 1803

In this book, we have presented two broad areas of human existence: sleep and dreaming. Both of these areas deal with the broader subject of consciousness and the absence of normal conscious awareness. Both relate in many ways to our physical and psychological health, yet the subjects are also vastly different. The early chapters describe sleep from the perspective of events taking place in the brain. It is based on objective, rigorous scientific studies that used sophisticated recording equipment. The presentation of dreams, on the other hand, strays beyond the limitations of scientific objectivity. Dreams are, by definition, subjective and, once research explores beyond events in the brain, the material becomes vague and even suspect to those seeking scientific objectivity (see "A Dream Product" box). This is not surprising: At one time, psychology as a scientific discipline completely dismissed subjective experiences to focus exclusively on observable, easily measurable behaviors. Here, too, the reader must accept that the information presented is often based more on clinical experience and intuition than on established fact. For all our technology, hu-

A Dream Product

In Xanadu did Kubla Khan

A stately pleasure-dome decree:

Where Alph, the sacred river, ran

Through caverns measureless to man

Down to a sunless sea.

—Samuel Taylor Coleridge, "Kubla Khan"

In 1797, the British Romantic poet Coleridge fell asleep while reading an account of a palace built by 13th-century Mongol Emperor of China, Kubla Khan. Reportedly, he slept for three hours and dreamed 200 to 300 lines of the above poem. On awakening, he took pen and ink and set down more than 50 lines. He was then interrupted on business for about an hour and, when he returned to his writing, found he could no longer remember the rest of the poem. He intended to complete the fragmented poem without the aid of his dream visions but never did so.

man experience cannot be totally explained on the basis of nerve impulses, blips on an EEG, or chemical reactions.

HEALTH AND SLEEP

People are generally unaware of the importance of sleep to good health. Sleep experts such as William Dement and Christopher Vaughan suggested that undiagnosed sleep disorders may underlie many medical conditions, including heart failure. Sleep debt has been shown to compromise the immune system, increasing vulnerability to serious medical conditions. Less dramatic is the possibility that millions of people may be functioning under conditions of fatigue, thus detracting from the quality of their lives. It has been estimated that we sleep about an hour and a half less than our grandparents did. Dement and Vaughan reported that at least half of the American population mismanages their sleep to the point of seriously affecting their health.

The generalizations about sleep cycles and rhythms outlined in Chapter 2 are based on large studies but do not help you determine your own sleep needs. People differ in the amount of time they require for optimal maintenance of their health. Sleep is important enough to justify the effort to determine how much sleep you actually need. One strategy is to determine the time it takes to fall asleep. Dement and Vaughan recommended a simple method: When you lie down to sleep, lightly grasp a spoon while holding your hand over, but not touching, a saucer. Just before closing your eyes, note the time. As you drift off to sleep, the spoon will drop onto the saucer. Unless you are seriously sleep deprived, the sound of the spoon clanging onto the saucer should wake you up. Again, note the time and calculate the time it took to fall asleep. Doing this each night for several days will provide a fairly accurate record of how sleepy you were. The shorter the duration (latency) of sleep onset, the more tired you were and the more you needed sleep. You can also try varying your bedtime for several nights and then note how tired you feel the next day. Do you find yourself nodding off when you should be studying?

Dement and Vaughan suggested the use of the seven-point Stanford Sleepiness Scale several times a day to measure how tired you feel. You can also keep a sleep diary for documenting your sleep latencies and daily level of sleepiness during various activities. The diary should record the time you go to bed, the hour you awaken, your sleep latency, the number of times you wake up during the night, the number and length of naps you take during the day, and the total number of hours you sleep each day. If you find you have a serious sleep debt—for example, you find that you are consistently falling asleep within five to ten minutes of lying down—you should make a determined effort to get more sleep. If those efforts fail, you need to accept that you may have a sleep disorder and see your doctor (see "Stanford Sleepiness Scale" box).

Standard Sleepiness Scale

William Dement and Christopher Vaughan suggest that you keep track of how sleepy you feel several times a day. Using the following seven-point scale, make a notation of the number that best describes how you feel:

1. Feeling active, vital, alert, and wide awake.
2. Functioning at a high level, not at peak.
3. Relaxed, not full alertness, responsive.
4. A little foggy, not at peak, let down.
5. Tired, losing interest, slowed down.
6. Drowsy, prefer to be lying down.
7. Nodding off, hard to stay awake.

Source: Dement, W. C., and C. Vaughan. *The Promise of Sleep.* New York: Dell Publishing, 337.

WHO ARE YOU?

Adolescence is a time when a person often struggles with definitions of self. In this book, you have been asked to think beyond your normal conscious experience and include your dreaming experiences, to abandon a concept of self as consistent in favor of one that has cycles, and to consider the interactions of both a biological and a psychological self. Attention to your dreams may convince you that your personality has a hidden dimension that is unknown to your conscious awareness, yet able to emerge in dreams in strange ways that require deciphering. Furthermore, this book has asked you to explore this submerged self to learn who you really are and to tap these resources for greater insight and self-awareness. In this concluding chapter, we ask you to consider who you are, both as a person and as a member of the human race. Your role as a waking and sleeping organism and one capable of having, interpreting, and using dreams provides one part of the answer to this question.

USING DREAMS FOR GAINING SELF-UNDERSTANDING AND ACHIEVING POTENTIAL

Self-awareness does not automatically change your behavior or improve your life. You need to develop an action plan to use insights that you derive from your dreams to best advantage. Developing such a plan requires taking stock of the major themes of your dreams, as well as the feelings associated with them. This can include sources of guilt, sadness, anger, fear, and anxiety. It also requires developing a realistic picture of your needs, hopes, and wishes; establishing goals; formulating realistic plans to achieve those goals; and, finally, building support systems to help you move ahead. Your personality picture can be clarified by asking yourself to identify the significant figures in your dream. Do they provide support or are they the source of a problem? What type of dream activities do you engage in? How do people react to you in your dreams? Are they accepting or rejecting? What characteristics do the people in your dreams display? To what degree would you attribute these characteristics to your waking self? Remember, every character in the dream may be you. Share your dreams with others and note their reactions. Create new endings to your dream that are more satisfying to you (see "Dreams and Creativity" box). A father dreamed that his 15-year-old daughter ran away from home after failing a science exam. He retold the dream, depicting himself as sympathizing with his daughter,

Dreams and Creativity

Are people who can recall, describe, or write down their own dreams more creative? Several studies seem to indicate that this is, indeed, the case. In 1995, M. Schredl administered a verbal creativity test to 44 young adults. The test had many parts, including a section that asked the subject to list as many words as possible with a specific word beginning, a specific ending, or a certain word characteristic. Other parts of the test measured interest in certain creative activities such as modeling with clay, creating a new recipe, or writing poetry. The subjects were also asked to rate their own creativity on a 5-point scale and to estimate the number of dreams they could recall over the past few months.

The score on the verbal creativity test was significantly related to the frequency of dream recall. Likewise, people who reported that they had creative interests also recalled more dreams. The strongest relationship of dream recall was with an interest in painting. The author believes that good dream recall requires both visual and verbal abilities.

Source: Schredl, M. "Creativity and Dream Recall." *Journal of Creative Behavior* 29 (1995): 16–24.

expressing confidence that she will do better next time, and offering to help her improve her study habits.

The productive use of dreams may require resources you do not currently possess. You may need to take courses to improve skills you would like to have. You may have to learn special techniques to reduce anxiety or control depression, improve communication skills, or improve study habits. Developing such strategies may require professional counseling or psychotherapy or even family therapy. Once a dream has proven helpful, it is important to keep it alive. Write it down and continue to look for new meanings. While dreams are not prophetic, sometimes you can make a dream come true if it reflects a significant wish.

DANGER SIGNALS

Dreams can provide a warning when something is seriously wrong. As you become more sensitive to your dreams and begin to maintain a written dream collection, you will likely notice some patterns and consistencies. The dreams may differ in content but express the same themes repeatedly. Day-to-day occurrences and concerns appear. Other dreams might express deep wishes and fantasies. You may also find yourself dreaming of unpleasant situations that are accompanied by negative emotions. When such dreams become frequent and predominate, it is important to question why and do something about it. This chapter deals with three negative emotions that may appear in dreams. Anxiety, depression, and anger are part of the human condition. Since they are with us during waking hours, they will also surface in dreams.

Anxiety

Anxiety, or stress, is a feeling very similar to fear. It can be protective by alerting us to possible danger. Too much of it can be destructive, interfering with clear thinking and effective action. Usually, we know what frightens us—encountering a three-foot-long snake, for example. Anxiety is less specific. You may not be quite sure what is bothering you. You can usually avoid things that frighten you, but anxiety stays with you. There are bodily changes associated with anxiety, such as a rapid heartbeat, sweaty palms, and a dry mouth. Many of these changes prepare the body for emergencies. Blood is shunted from the digestive organs to the brain and muscles, for example, allowing us to defend ourselves or escape. The hormone **adrenaline**, which is secreted by the adrenal gland in times of crisis, produces these changes. There is also a feeling that something bad is about to happen. In extreme cases, the person feels as if he or she is going crazy or is about to die— this is called **panic**. The body reacts as if there is an emergency even though no crisis currently exists. Anxiety can interfere with thinking and disrupt concentration. Extreme anxiety during an exam will wipe out everything you have studied the night before. When anxiety persists over a long period, it can compromise your immune system and make you more susceptible to disease. It can also produce a number of serious psychological conditions called anxiety disorders. The exact mechanism by which this occurs is unknown, but the conversion of anxiety to symptoms is believed to involve a biological predisposition, the effects of learning, and an environmental trigger. Symptoms may include excessive worrying, compulsive rituals such as repeated handwashing, specific fears, general fearfulness, shyness, and avoidance of social situations. Anxiety is one of the reactions to trauma. Post-traumatic stress disorder includes symptoms of heightened vigilance (always being on guard), and nightmares and flashbacks of the original trauma, which seem to be real. All of these conditions require professional help.

Anxiety dreams involve the experience of a vague apprehension about the future. The dreamer anticipates some danger, but the source of that danger is unknown. He or she is poised for action but does not know how to act. A test-taking situation is a common example. The dreamer knows there will be a test but does not know the specific questions to study. Separation from loved ones is another example. Anxiety dreams include running away from something menacing like aliens or monsters, being tested and failing, and being unprepared or inappropriate. One teenager dreamed of wearing a wedding gown to a rock concert and being ridiculed. An adult man had recurrent dreams of flooding water, losing his car, and being attacked by enemy soldiers whenever he was stressed.

Traumatic dreams replay some horrible event we have experienced. They require little interpretation, as they are usually accurate reproductions of the original experience. Nightmares are frightening dreams in which the individual experiences a sense of dread, difficulty in breathing, and a sense of paralysis. Some therapists have interpreted nightmares as a conflict between some desire and an anticipated punishment for fulfilling that desire. The main emotion is terror. Nightmares are relatively rare; some people never experience them. They may reflect a concern about some upcoming event (see "Stress and Dreams" box).

Depression

Depression can be mild or very serious. It involves an overwhelming sense of guilt, helplessness, and profound sadness. A depressed person is so preoccupied with these feelings that he or she may be unable to cope with the requirements of everyday living. Just as these feelings affect waking life, they also appear as the content of dreams. We all have ups and downs in our emotional life. Clinical depression can also be cyclical, but is a very serious condition because, at its worst, it can lead to self-destructive behavior. Sometimes it hides beneath the surface, only to produce crying spells, loss of appetite and weight loss or overeating and weight gain, fatigue, loss of interest in life, withdrawal from people, a sense of hopelessness, and suicidal thoughts and intentions. Depression always involves damage to

Stress and Dreams

The Vietnam War produced serious and long-lasting emotional problems in those who saw combat. A 1990 study by C. A. Cook, R. D. Caplan, and H. Wolowitz collected data from 442 men who were eligible for military duty during this war. One group had been in combat; the other had not. The subjects were asked to report their dreams and any nightmares that they had during the past three months. They were also questioned about any stressful experiences during childhood and adolescence, including life-threatening health problems, parental problems, and exposure to violence.

Both groups reported 3.5 times as many pleasant dreams as nightmares. Of those who had seen heavy combat in Vietnam, 32% reported nightmares, whereas 16% of those with no combat experience reported nightmares. The content of their nightmares included themes of death, injury, personal loss, and difficulties at work. A history of illness, injury, or parental problems during childhood and adolescence did not relate to the frequency of nightmares reported. Involvement in violent behavior, on the other hand, was related to a high frequency of nightmares. Subjects who had seen combat in Vietnam had a high frequency of nightmares. Combat experience was unrelated to the number of pleasant dreams reported.

This and other studies support the notion that frightening dreams occur in response to exposure to stressful life events, particularly violent events. It follows that the use of dream content to identify emotional problems related to psychological stress is a meaningful approach in treatment.

Source: Cook, C. A., R. D. Caplan, and H. Wolowitz. "Nonwaking Responses to Waking Stressors: Dreams and Nightmares." *Journal of Applied Social Psychology* 3 (1990): 199–206.

self-esteem. We tend to blame ourselves for anything bad that happens, seldom taking credit for good things. We overreact to bad events, magnifying their importance, and believing they will last forever. Bad events cannot be avoided, however: Deaths, separations, divorce of parents, illnesses, rejection, and failure happen to everyone. It is how we react to these events that reflects whether or not we are depressed.

University of Pennsylvania psychologist Martin Seligman has shown that attitudes of helplessness and optimism can be learned. People who develop chronic feelings of helplessness in response to negative events are prone to depression. Those who maintain a positive attitude are less likely to become depressed, are less prone to illness, and tend to enjoy longer lives and more success.

Depression reveals itself in dreams. A doctoral dissertation by J.M.C. Galley in 1994 studied the dreams of ninth through twelfth grade high school students and found significant differences between girls who were depressed and those who were not. The depressed group reported dreams in which the dreamer had a lack of control over dream events. Someone else in the dream determined both what was taking place and the dream event's outcome. Typical themes were "my grandfather died," "my car was stolen," "I failed English," and "my plane was hijacked." Dreams of nondepressed girls revealed a feeling of internal control: "I studied real hard and aced the exam."

John Maltzberger of the Boston Psychoanalytic Society and Hospital in 1993 compared dreams of people who were suicidally depressed and those whose depression was not suicidal. Since both groups were depressed, any differences found were assumed to result from the basis of suicidal ideas and intent. Dreams of the suicidal group showed more death imagery and violent content. Death and suicide were seen as satisfactory resolutions to pain and conflict. Suicidal themes were sometimes expressed directly in the manifest dream content.

Anger

The third danger signal in dreams is anger. Anger happens. It is what we feel when we are frustrated in reaching an important goal or when we are unfairly criticized. It may be directed at friends, relatives, teachers, or employers. We may even direct it at ourselves. Often, the anger is justified. A supervisor embarrasses you in front of your coworkers. You would love to tell her off, but that would make matters worse, so you say nothing and seethe inside.

Anger hurts. Some people live by the credo "I don't get angry; I get even." These people are not being truthful. They waste time planning revenge, time that could have been used far more productively. Unchecked, anger can become rage and rage can become hate. Anger can fester until it clouds your perceptions and pushes you to act in ways that are destructive and self-defeating. Management of anger is difficult. It requires that you act constructively to confront whatever situation is making you angry, assert yourself, and try to fix whatever went wrong.

Dreams of destruction, violence, and revenge all express anger. In the dream, you may be the punisher or the victim. Consider this violent dream of an 18-year-old male, reported by psychologists Robert K. Winegar and Ross Levin at the Albert Einstein College of Medicine in 1997:

I was in a pool hall shooting pool with my friend. Then, suddenly, I saw some kids jump him, about ten of them. I then took a cue stick and started swinging. I took eight of them down, breaking their bones. The other two were still beating my friend when I drove the end into the head of one of them, breaking my stick in the process. The other guy pulled out a knife. In my fury, I drove the shortened stick into the guy's left eye, thus killing him. I picked up my friend and started to flee. However, the police were already outside and began to cuff me.

You do not need to be a psychologist to see a warning sign here. It would be important for the dreamer to trace his associations and identify the trigger in real life. Is there some nonviolent way to address the frustration? Often, it is because we are underassertive that we set up a frustrating situation. It is important to be able to say "no" when you mean "no." Learning to be honest in relationships, to speak up when someone has slighted you, may prevent anger later on. Clearing the air is a wonderful tonic for angry feelings. You will not get your way in all your confrontations, but you will feel better for having tried. Learn to be selective in your relationships and to avoid unreasonable people whenever possible.

Other Conditions

In 1995, Susan M. Brink, John A. B. Allen, and Walter Boldt, psychologists at the University of British Columbia, analyzed the dreams of a group of young women with eating disorders and compared them with the dreams of women without eating disorders. Women in the eating disorder group had a higher number of dreams that reflected a sense of ineffectiveness and self-hate. There was also a preoccupation with food and weight.

Recurrent dreams are thought to indicate some unsolved problem. Some psychologists believe that recurrent dreams may feature images and experiences that do not fit well into already established memories and thoughts. In a study by C. Rycroft in 1979, common recurrent dream events included taking an exam, running to catch a train, finding an unknown room in one's house, traveling in a strange city, and being threatened by a tidal wave.

DREAMS AND LIFE STAGES

Dreams vary according to one's stage of life. Psychologists recognize that each stage of development brings conflicts of a different nature. Infants and babies need to learn to trust adults to satisfy their physical needs (food, warmth, protection) and their emotional needs (affection, security). If these needs are not met consistently, the infant or baby will learn to mistrust others. Toddlers are rapidly learning motor skills and how to be independent. If they are not allowed some freedom to do so, they will continue to feel dependent. Battles with parents over socialization and toilet training are bound to occur and to influence dreams. From ages three to five, children are expected to incorporate self-control over their behavior. They develop the mechanism of guilt when they have done something wrong. Internal conflicts occur between doing what they want to do and what parents define as allowable behavior. In this way, the child learns to regulate his or her own behavior in ways that are acceptable to society. When the child enters school, he or she must learn to handle schoolwork. Skills in building, crafts, sports, and household tasks also develop. If children encounter frequent failure, criticism, or rejection in learning these skills, instead of learning to feel competent, they learn a sense of inferiority.

From ages 11 to 18, the child must gain a sense of who he or she is. This is called identity. Teenagers try out many roles and behavior, not all of which are acceptable to adults. Outlandish hairstyles, clothing, tattoos, and body piercing are some examples. This is generally a very difficult time for teenagers, which some experts have labeled an "**identity crisis**." The manner in which teenagers resolve these crises has a marked influence on later adult stages of development.

Adults have needs as well. These include the need to produce in work situations, to advance professionally, to earn a living, to engage in meaningful social relationships, and—for some—to marry and have children. As they grow older, adults have concerns about caring for family and loved ones. They worry about the health and safety of their children and eventually about their own health and the prospect of death.

Calvin S. Hall (1909–1985), a cognitive psychologist who spent most of his career teaching at Case Western Reserve University, studied the dreams of hundreds of people and classified them into several categories: conflicts between parents and children that involve alliances and competition; freedom versus security; moral conflicts; sex role conflicts; and life and death. Teenagers were most likely to experience dreams related to identity conflicts but also had dreams reflecting earlier developmental stages.

The dreams of preschool children are often scary. From age three to five, nightmares and night terrors are common. Children may wake up screaming. They have trouble distinguishing between dreams and reality. Their dreams are of monsters, giants, and witches who threaten them. These images may represent their parents, who threaten their initiative and punish their aggressive behavior. It is likely that children's fairy tales provide content for dreams. The wolf in *Little Red Riding Hood* has endured for centuries in children's literature, perhaps because it expresses basic fears of young children.

The dreams of school-age children may include disguised images of teachers whom they perceive as cruel. Feelings of inferiority, humiliation, and failure may appear in dreams. The child who is unable to learn to read as fast as his or her classmates, or who is inhibited socially or taunted by peers, may relive these failures in dreams.

Adolescence is a time of disengagement from parents when feelings of alienation are common. Teenagers react through nonconformity and sometimes noncompliance with rules and customs. Dreams of alienation occur frequently as teenagers seek to define their identity. These dreams may take the form of being asked who they are and being unable to answer, or being asked for an ID card and being unable to find it. Another common theme is wearing a mask or being in disguise. Dreams of examination often involve reliving a test that has already been passed. The dream seems to reassure the dreamer that he or she will also succeed on an upcoming exam. The dream may also express an insecurity that the dreamer did not deserve to pass the previous exam and will have to retake it. At a deeper level, the dream may signify rites of passage as the adolescent approaches the responsibilities of adulthood. A frequent teen dream involves a competition between the dreamer and the same-sexed parent for the attention of the opposite-sexed parent. Such dreams can occur at any time but are more frequent during adolescence.

GENDER DIFFERENCES

Males and females have different dreams (see "Gender Differences in Dreams" box). Male dreams are more action-oriented and more aggressive than those of females. Boys dream of fighting, playing sports, and traveling to far-off lands. Girls may be more sensitive to verbal and nonverbal cues, emotions, and social relationships in their dreams. Menstrual dreams occur in girls and women. The specific form of the dream will depend upon the dreamer's attitude toward her period. For some, menstrual dreams may reflect a desire for fertility; for others they represent concerns or even revulsion about blood.

Dreams that result in orgasm are common in both males and females. So called "wet dreams" in males occur most often during adolescence when sexual outlets for relief of sexual tension are lacking. Females also experience orgasm in dreams. Erotic dreams often involve anxiety related to sexual behavior, especially if such behavior violates parental, religious, and moral values.

Additional dreams that are typical at different life stages are presented in Appendix 2.

WHAT IS REALITY?

Until the early part of the 20th century, psychologists confined their study of personality to conscious awareness. Neurologists assumed that nothing important occurred in the brain during sleep. Dreams were regarded either as noise in the nervous system or were dismissed as the domain of mystics, prophets, and fortune-tellers. Dreams and reality were sharply separated. Those who did study dreams and dreaming were suspect. To-

Gender Differences in Dreams

Age is not the only determinant of differences in dream content. Differences in roles and expectations placed upon boys and girls, as well as inborn biological differences, usually result in separate and distinct male and female identities. It would be expected that the dreams of both genders also would reflect such differences. In 1966, C. Hall and R. J. Van de Castle found that the dreams of females more frequently featured people, emotions, and social interactions than did the dreams of males. The dreams of males, on the other hand, contained more aggressive interactions, more often in unfamiliar, outdoor settings than the dreams of females.

R. K. Winegar and R. Levin studied the dreams of 115 adolescents of both sexes, aged 15 to 18. According to their 1997 report, regardless of age, females' dreams were longer and their reports used more words. Their dreams were more attuned to subtle verbal and nonverbal cues. They used phrases such as "I understand . . . ," "I am aware . . . ," "I recognize. . . ." The males' dreams were more action-oriented and more aggressive. They were less likely to address intimate interpersonal issues. These results may reflect basic personality differences between the genders in our culture.

day, we recognize that there is more to personality than is apparent and that the sleeping brain is far from inactive. Just as the fantasy and science fiction of yesterday dealt with matters —such as cloning organisms and space travel—that have become technological reality today, so have sleep and dreams also found new relevance.

This book has expressed a belief in the meaning of dreams, just as all of our existence has meaning. Without disputing the importance of neurological underpinnings, dreams must be more than random firings of nerve cells. They are a product of the dreamer's memory, history, experiences, and learning. However obscure their meaning, they are the productions of the dreamer and assume the dreamer's reality. To the dreamer, the dream is real. The Chinese philosopher Chuang Tzu, quoted at the beginning of this chapter, was implying that there are two realities, in dreams and awakened states, even though they are markedly different. Dement and Vaughan suggested that the reason we forget dreams is so we do not become confused between dreams and reality. The brain provides an internal representation of reality, and all our awareness of what is real is limited to what is interpreted by the brain. Are we, then, to devalue the reality of dreams because they do not obey the logical rules of our waking lives? Does evidence of the neurological events that accompany dreams explain them, or merely define them?

We have adhered to contemporary, cognitive explanations of dreams, while acknowledging that there are levels of conscious awareness and that a large part of our experiences and memories often lie outside of immediate recall. Orthodox psychoanalytic theory holds that an active unconscious motivates much of our behavior and that a vigilant "**censor**" serves as a gatekeeper, barring threatening aggressive, destructive, and sexual thoughts from reaching consciousness. Here, instead of invoking such deviousness to the personality, we seek explanations in known physiological and psychological explanations. Associations and memories, even those not immediately available to us in a waking state, provide the resource for dream content.

As members of a culture, we tend to cling to our heritage of myths and legends. We would like to believe that magicians read minds, predict the future, and communicate with the dead. Yet, our science leads us to avoid what seems to border on the mystical or magical in favor of the simplest mechanisms to account for our dream life. Taken at face value, dreams tell us less than we already knew. They express an inefficient, roundabout, sometimes metaphorical distortion of the information we have accumulated in our memory. Interpreted by tracing our associations, dreams have the potential to reveal what we were not previously aware we knew or did not fully appreciate. They catalog our concerns, recognize our wishes, give voice to our fears, and sometimes uncover motivations that energize and direct our behavior. In this view, dreams are not magical pathways to a mystical, powerful, and destructive unconscious, but a means to explore what has gone before, what is already there, and what we can possibly use to solve problems, plan our future, and reach our goals. There are no little people inside us, fighting over our psyche, directing upward traffic to our thoughts, or forcing us to forget what is scary or upsetting. Dreams have psychological meaning but not deep psychological purpose. Whether they are used purposefully depends upon the dreamer. Dreams are intrinsically interesting. People who like riddles, puzzles, and word games will like the challenge of dream interpretation as well.

SLEEP, DREAMS, AND THE HUMAN CONDITION

As the most advanced members of the animal kingdom, we possess the capacity to explore our thoughts, examine ourselves, plan for our futures, and seek meaning in life. Some animals have REM sleep and may also dream. It is unlikely, however, that any organism other than the human being has the capacity to analyze its dreams and to contemplate their significance. Our lives can be reduced to stages, phases, cycles, rhythms, habits, and nerve impulses and chemical reactions. However, such abstractions reveal only the external manifestations of our existence, not our inner thoughts, feelings, values, or spirituality. That our conscious awareness exists at all is nothing short of miraculous. With all our knowledge of bodily processes and advanced scientific technology, we cannot explain consciousness. No less astounding is the fact that our sleep, so important to our health, includes REM sleep, which we appear to need, and that REM sleep produces dreams. Is this, after all, the purpose of sleep? Dreams reflect our role as thinking, feeling organisms, in sleep as well as waking states. Contemporary physicists have attempted to find a universal explanation linking every aspect of our existence, from the smallest particles of matter to the entire cosmos. The concept of a unity of mind and matter, as asserted by Aristotle, is consistent with this thinking. Sleep is not divorced from waking life but is part of a continuous cycle. The subjective experiences that we call dreams are not the isolated ramblings of a brain turned off; they connect in meaningful ways to conscious preoccupations, recent events, distant memories, and strivings that we may not fully address in waking life.

Sleep does not automatically bring health. Dreams do not automatically lead to happiness. People who retreat entirely into their dreams are regarded as mentally ill. Dreams are linked to reality and are useful only in that perspective. Sleep and dreaming are natural processes, not mystical experiences. Exploring the meaning of these sleep-time visions is consistent with the broader process of seeking self-understanding. We have only scratched the surface of sleep and dreams in this book. You may wish to explore more about the biology of sleep and dreams, dream analysis, and the use of dreams in psychotherapy. Do not lose your enthusiasm for the place of sleep and dreams in your understanding about psychology and the workings of the brain.

Dream on.

The future belongs to those who believe in the beauty of their dreams.

—Eleanor Roosevelt, First Lady of the United States
(1918–1962)

■ **Learn more about the dreams and your life** Search the Internet for *dream analysis.*

Appendices

Appendix 1

INTERPRETATION OF DREAMS

It has never been my object to record my dreams, just the determination to realize them.

—Man Ray, American artist and photographer,
1890–1976

The process of deriving meaning from dreams requires three steps: collection, recording, and analysis. We offer a brief discussion here of how these are done. You might try it with your own dreams, with the understanding that it is not a substitute for psychotherapy or other professional help. The method presented here is consistent with the cognitive approach of Dr. Clara Hill at the University of Maryland. It has been modified here to adapt it for a teenage audience.

COLLECTING AND RECORDING DREAMS

Collection is the hardest part because you will forget dreams almost as soon as you wake up unless you make an immediate effort to write them down. This is doubly hard in the middle of the night, though it is certainly possible if you keep a pad and paper by your bed. Even so, most of the dreams you collect will probably be those you had just before awakening. You will not always be successful in recording your dreams, but you will improve with practice. Bear in mind that your recollection may not always be accurate. Freud believed that people remember only a tiny fragment of their dreams, even with great effort. This should not bother you, since it is your associations to the dream that will be significant.

Recording the dream should be done as soon as possible after recall to prevent forgetting more of the dream images. After writing out the dream in as much detail as possible, construct a chart to classify it and begin the process of analysis. First, give the dream a title that reflects the dream story—"Lost in a strange city," for example. In the first column, list all the dream images—people, places, objects, and activities. You should include them in order of appearance. Include descriptive adjectives as they come to you, such as "hairy gorilla." The second column requires a brief summary of the action depicted in association with each image—for example, "I'm taking my SATs."

The third column is reserved for your associations to the image and action. Hold nothing back and do no editing, no matter how silly or insignificant your associations may seem. Be spontaneous. If nothing comes to mind, proceed to the next image. If you bring up a chain of associations, write them all down. Your associations may include some memory that you had not thought about for a long time. Ask yourself pertinent questions: What do sunglasses remind me of? What do ice cream cones mean to me? Did anything related to soccer balls happen to me recently? Do I refer to Big Macs® by any other name?

The last column is reserved for any emotions you recall having in response to any parts of the dream. You may not remember any emotions but you may feel emotion merely in recalling the dream. A strong emotion that goes along with a seemingly insignificant dream event may mean it was not so insignificant after all.

The sequence of events may be important. Remember, dreams are condensed. Often, a dream element relates back to a previous part of the dream. One teenager typically had two-part dreams. In the first part, something frightening or upsetting would happen. It might be a problem that the dreamer could not control when awake. The second part of the dream would typically be some success or accomplishment—a self-comforting thought. When awake, the teenager frequently told himself some positive thought after experiencing a disappointment or failure. In his dreams, he did the same thing. It was as if he were saying to himself: "I have handled bad situations before. This is no catastrophe."

ANALYZING DREAMS

You now know the basic elements for interpreting dreams. Remember, all the parts of your dream relate to you and your associations and memories. Usually, there is no intention to produce a dream. Lucid dreams, which some people can induce, are one exception to this generalization (see Chapter 1). Previously learned associations result in one thought leading to another. Tracing these connections may reveal motives that are ordinarily beyond your level of awareness. Most people are too occupied with everyday life to address deep issues. Dream analysis may provide new meanings to old ideas. Perhaps there will be no new revelations but instead a more structured and crystallized picture of yourself. This new awareness is what we refer to as "**insight**." It may change the way you understand an important part of your world.

Assume that all the parts of the dream are connected. Take nothing at face value. Remember, ideas are condensed; people and objects may not be as they appear. Be sensitive to symbols and metaphors. Emotions may be attached to the wrong meaning. Suppose a purple cow in the dream reminds you of a hideous gift from your aunt Betty. Replace the cow with Aunt Betty in the story. Does it make more sense now? Is there something that has been bothering you about Aunt Betty, perhaps her purple eye shadow?

Consider the dream in light of what is currently going on in your life. Perhaps Aunt Betty is coming to visit and will be sleeping in your room. In the dream, you may be doing something that you would never do in reality. Is it what you would really like to do? What would happen if you did as you dreamed? Are you harboring a secret wish?

Explore the dream with regard to past memories. In dreams, we tend to relive situations that we did not handle well—situations we never dealt with adequately. Dreams can have multiple meanings. Several meanings may be valid. Remember, dreams condense meanings. Sometimes, two dreams occur close together. The first may express a problem, the second a possible solution. Ask yourself why you had that particular dream and why you had it now. It could be an insignificant event, yet still have meaning. Was it something you need to do?

Dreams may lead you to examine contradictions within your personality. Great novels intrigue us because the characters are not one-dimensional. No one is all good or all bad. No one is driven by only one motive. Sometimes you play the role of a protective parent, sometimes the rebellious child, and sometimes the clown. The dream allows you to recognize the various and often contradictory roles you play in life. Some therapists believe that every character in the dream is some part of you. You can accept these roles, discard some of them, or integrate them into your personality.

Attempting to analyze your own dream is a complicated undertaking. You may not always be right. Some dreams mean nothing. Consider your interpretations as hypotheses to be tested in waking life. You may want to discuss your dreams with your parents or with a trained professional.

Photocopy this page and use it to keep track of your dreams.

DREAM CHART

Date: _____

Circumstances: _____

Title: _____

Dream sequence: _____

_____

_____

_____

_____

Dream elements	Action	Associations	Feelings
(people, objects, places)	(What's happening?)		

_____

_____

_____

_____

_____

Dream meaning: _____

Retell the dream sequence, reflecting its meaning: _____

_____

_____

Insights _____

_____

_____

Action suggested: _____

_____

TYPICAL DREAMS

A teenage boy had the following dream:

> I am on a train. It is taking me somewhere I do not want to go. There are other people on the train, but I feel that I am alone. The train enters a long, dark tunnel. It seems like the tunnel will never end. I feel trapped.

The boy had several associations to the dream. The first was being on a train each summer going to camp. He did not like summer camp. He did not relate well to the other children. He felt that his parents were just trying to get rid of him for the summer. His association to the tunnel was darkness and being alone in the dark—a fear he had as a young child. He recalled a childhood experience of crawling into a large drainpipe near his home. He had taken a dare and entered the pipe. After going about 25 feet, he became frightened and turned back.

The dream occurred just prior to his parents' departure on a trip to Europe. He was supposed to stay with his grandmother. It was also close to the time when he would be leaving for college for the first time. Both situations made him feel insecure. His parents would not be there for him if he needed them. The dream had meaning on two levels. His parents' travel plans aroused an early fear of separation. Leaving for college also aroused this fear, but this fear triggered another fearful memory, related to small, dark, enclosed places. He did not dream of sewage tunnels but, rather, of a train ride through a dark tunnel. The train expressed the meaning of separation from his parents. His present concerns brought back the more powerful fears from his childhood.

Once the boy saw the connection between two instances of separation from his parents and his emotional reaction, he was able to discuss his fears with his parents. They made arrangements to call him at specific times and to e-mail him from Europe. The same strategy also reassured him that he could handle living at an out-of-town college.

An 18-year-old girl also had a train dream:

> I am riding to class on an elevated train. The train stops at a station and my father gets on, but instead of sitting next to me, he chooses a seat some distance away. I am hurt and angry. I get off the train at the next stop, even though it is not my station. I know I will be late for class.

The girl's associations led her to realize that she had always sought her father's approval, but never felt she had gained it. She believed she could gain it only by academic achievement, which would elevate her in her father's eyes. Her feelings of rejection are indicated by her father's avoidance of her, even though she was on her way to class. Leaving the train was an act of defiance. Discussion of the dream with a therapist convinced her that she did not need her father's approval. She could make her own decisions about what was important to her. She was able to discuss the dream with her father and began to work through her issues with him.

A man was scheduled for surgery after tearing a tendon in his shoulder. The night before his operation he had the following "worry" dream:

> I am riding a motorcycle to an appointment. I must not be late. Now I am driving my car. Suddenly I cannot see. My hat has fallen down over my eyes. Yet I cannot remove the hat. I drive blind for a short distance, but realize I must stop or risk hitting someone. I pull the car

> over and stop. I exit the car and find that I am in a hotel
> lobby. I leave the car and do some business in the hotel.
> When I return I find that my car is gone. The hotel clerk
> explains that it has been impounded. The hotel will not
> give me back my car.

Associations to the dream suggest that the motorcycle and the car were related to concerns about arriving at the hospital on time. He related motorcycles to instances of traumatic head injury from motorcycle accidents. There was ambivalence about having the surgery—a desire to restore function in his arm but fear of the operation. This was partially an explanation of stopping the car. Like the motorcycle, anesthesia during surgery had some degree of risk attached to it. But the image of his hat over his eyes referred back to a previous surgery for a retinal detachment. The man had lost vision in the affected eye. It was as if a window shade had been pulled down over the eye. The concern about hitting someone was related to the cause of the shoulder tear, hitting and pitching a baseball. The hotel represented the hospital. They both begin with the same letter. Doing business at the hotel represented the surgery. Doing his business was, of course, the surgery, but the man had also had the thought that the orthopedic surgeon did a good business repairing shoulders. The disappearing car was an expression of the fear he had during the retinal surgery that he would not be able to drive again and would have to sell his car. Even the present operation would require a suspension of driving for a few weeks while his shoulder healed. He had said to his wife that he thought he could drive with one arm. She had joked, in return, that she would hide his car keys.

A woman had the following dream after her mother-in-law died of cancer. The woman was on vacation with her own mother and daughter.

> I am walking on the beach in a somewhat remote area
> where I had not walked before. My mother-in-law is sit-
> ting on a bench. It seemed very real. She has her real
> hair (not the wig she wore after chemo). She says, "Isn't
> this a beautiful place?"

The dream was so vivid that the woman returned to the same spot the next day. The sound of her mother-in-law's voice was so real she could recall it in her wakened state. The meaning of the dream requires little interpretation. The woman missed her loved one and hoped that she, too, was in a beautiful place.

A 40-year-old woman had a work-related dream:

> I am driving my car. In the rearview mirror I see anoth-
> er car approaching from the rear. The car is an
> Enterprise rent-a-car. I can see the big "E" on the side.
> The car is weaving all over the road. The car passes me.
> I keep on driving. The car now regains control and slows
> down as I approach it.

The woman's immediate supervisor at work is named Ed. He is a big man. He typically rents Enterprise cars for consultants. He has been harassing her. The woman believes that her supervisor is out of control. She fears for her own mental health but does not want to leave her job. The dream is also a wish fulfillment that both she and Ed will regain control.

DREAMS IN THERAPY: THREE CASE STUDIES

CARMEN

Carmen is a 17-year-old high school senior living with her father and stepmother. She sees a therapist because of an anxiety disorder that consists of generalized worrying and compulsive traits. Carmen relates a brief but troublesome dream:

> I am looking through a glass window. Behind the window is the Virgin Mary. She is carrying a cross. She looks very kind. I desperately want to be with her. I reach out to touch her, but the glass blocks me. I feel a sad longing.

Carmen interprets her dream as one representing a great religious need that remains unfulfilled. She forms associations to the glass, the Virgin Mary, and the cross. She indicates that she has a picture of the Virgin Mary on her nightstand. The picture is behind glass. She reveals a deep desire to be like the Virgin, to lead a life of perfection. At one time, she thought she would like to be a nun but now realizes she wants to be a perfect wife and mother.

Carmen was asked to explore her ideas of motherhood. She revealed that her biological mother died when she was four years old. She has only vague recollections about her, but her name was Mary. Carmen was never told any details about her mother's death. She has an intense desire to learn more about her mother, but her relatives refuse to discuss it. Carmen lived with an aunt for a few years when her father could not properly care for her. When her father remarried, she went to live with him and his new wife. Her stepmother is cold and distant. She provides for Carmen's needs, but Carmen believes that she ignores her emotionally. Carmen has felt imperfect all her life. She believes that she disappoints her stepmother and can never please her. She intends to live life to please others and to prove herself worthy. In treatment, she needs to learn that it is not necessary to be perfect. She must accept herself for who she is and demand respect from others.

MICHAEL

British psychoanalyst Jane Sayers introduced her 1998 book "Boy Crazy" with reference to Charles Dickens's first paragraph of *A Tale of Two Cities*. "It was the best of times; it was the worst of times." In it, she discusses Michael. Fifteen-year-old Michael's dreams graphically express the up-and-down feelings of the turbulence of adolescence.

Michael is in the eleventh grade. He has a history of depression and has been a loner in school. His parents are divorced, and he alternates between living with his mother during the week and his father on weekends. His mother tends to overcontrol and overprotect. He has trouble communicating with his father. Michael is a good student but typically does too much—more than is reasonable. He becomes very anxious as tests approach or assignments become due.

Michael has been in counseling for several months and has made considerable progress. He is no longer depressed. He has made some friends in school and is more confident about himself. He has negotiated with his mother to give him more space and has been successful. He held a summer job and now has a part-time job after school. The previous summer, he spent one week on a cruise to Nova Scotia with his father and stepmother and one week at the shore with his mother. Both of these experiences went well, he says.

The following two dreams occurred two weeks before returning to school in the fall. He had reported mild apprehension about the start of classes. He was worried that he would slip back into old patterns of worrying about grades and social isolation.

> I am swimming in the ocean. I am alone. There are huge waves. I am exhausted. I seem to be trying to get somewhere. No, I am running away from something. I am exhausted. I feel as if I can't swim another stroke. Then, in the distance, I see a rock. It is sticking up out of the water. I think that if I can make the rock I will be safe. I swim toward it. With my last breath, I make the rock and swim on to it. I am safe. I sit on the rock and try to catch my breath. I hear a woman's voice in the distance. This is weird because I am in the middle of the ocean. The voice is familiar but I can't place it. The voice says, "Come back. Get off the rock, but don't get your feet wet."

Michael was asked to associate to the parts of the dream. The main images, in addition to himself, were the ocean, swimming, the rock, and a woman's voice. Michael's associations to the ocean and swimming were negative. He has always had a fear of drowning and is not a strong swimmer. His parents are divorced and he spends several weeks each summer at the seashore with his father. His father had tried to persuade him to try out for the swim team, a suggestion that Michael ignored. It has been a source of contention for many years. Michael associated the rock with a feeling of stability and security. He brought up the phrases "solid as a rock," "the rock of Gibraltar," and "rock-and-roll." Michael escapes to his room when things get rough at home and listens to hard rock CDs through earphones, shutting out everything else.

Michael described his dream emotions as relief at reaching the rock and anger at hearing the voice. He remembers the voice as shrill, demanding, and irritating. He believes the voice could have been that of his mother. Michael explained that he was in a bind in the dream. Although he was safe on the rock, it was no solution. Eventually, he would have to leave and go back into the water. Yet, how could he save himself without getting wet? He recognized that his mother often gives him impossible commands —to be responsible but also independent. When he does something on his own, his mother worries that he is in danger. "She pushes me out with one hand and pulls me back with the other. I am between a rock and a hard place."

At this point, Michael seemed to be gaining some insight about his interactions with his mother. The dream seemed to express many typical teenage conflicts that relate to needs for independence without guilt or shame and the development of a sense of identity apart from one's parents. Michael was able to confront his mother about their relationship. She was willing to try to allow him more space to work out his problems, even risking failure.

The second dream involved Michael's mother and stepmother.

I am on a boat with my father, near the stern. We are on a river in a valley. The walls of it [the valley] rise up on each side of us. The waves of the river are very high, almost as high as the valley itself. There are windows at the back of the boat to look out, and my father has already gone to one. Whenever I am near the windows, I am afraid I will fall out, even though they are small. I go back into the boat into a casino. There is a counter in front of me. There are several packs of cards spread out. The person behind the counter tells me to take a deck. . . .

> Now I am on a battlefield, enemies all around. I am not exact-
> ly sure who is friend and who is foe. I am not sure which side
> of the battle I am on exactly, but I know well enough who my
> friends are. I have to fight some of the attackers. One of the
> people on my side gets wounded while I am doing that. The
> way I defeat my enemies is to stab them in the back with a
> spear. Or, if I get into a fight with one of them I try to hit them
> until I can find a chink in the armor.

Michael realized that his dream refers to the cruise with his father and stepmother. He was bored and wanted to read in his cabin. However, he felt there was something wrong with him for not wanting to be more involved in shipboard activities. His stepmother had told him that he would spend very little time in the cabin because there was so much to do on the ship. Until he related his dream, Michael did not realize that the cruise did not go as well as he had been telling himself. He now realized that there was a battle inside of him. The second part of the dream expresses this conflict, drawing images from a videogame Michael had played, called *The Thirteenth Warrior*. In this video, a poet is exiled to the land of the Vikings. He has to defend himself against the "Wendos," small people who believe they are bears. In the first part of the dream, Michael is afraid of falling out of small windows. When questioned about the ship windows, Michael indicated that he was afraid he would lose his glasses out those windows. Earlier that summer, he had been in a kayak with his dad. They were broadsided by a wave, and he actually did lose his glasses. He realized that he should not have been wearing them in the kayak. He feared his father would make him pay for replacing them. On another occasion, he lost his glasses on the lawn and ran over them with the mower. The kayak experience may explain the high waves in Michael's dream, threatening the boat. The words *falling out* have a double meaning. Michael saw the connection with the expression meaning to have a disagreement with someone. If he lost his glasses a third time, he would surely displease his father and stepmother, who were already annoyed at him for wishing to stay in the cabin. This prospect made him feel anxious.

The cruise ship did have a casino. Michael would have liked to gamble but could not because he was too young. He was not allowed to gamble just as he was not allowed to remain in his room. Michael recognized the double meaning of "deck" on a ship and the "deck of cards" he was handed in his dream. It was not a standard deck, he explained, but one from the game *Magic*, a game he played often at a recreation center in his neighborhood. In the game, there is pressure to get his deck ready. The ship's deck for Michael was also a place of risk and pressure. In fact, the dream reminded Michael of another game called *Risk*. The battlefield part of the dream was again associated with the game *Magic* and a video game called *Soul Reaper*, a battlefield situation. "Stab in the back" and "chink in the armor" both reflect Michael's own sense of vulnerability in his relationship with his father and stepmother. They also seem to reflect identity problems. Michael does not know which side he is on. He travels back and forth between his parents' two homes, not knowing where he belongs, whom to side with. If he is with his father, he risks alienating his mother (attack from the rear) and visa versa.

The two parts of the dream belong together. Michael's boat trip was filled with tension, when he would rather have been relaxing at home, reading, or playing video games. His stress was not confined to the cruise but was an everyday part of his life since his parents' divorce. He is torn in his loyalties. He cannot risk a falling out with his mother, father, or stepmother. He is always vulnerable, under siege. His life is a battlefield, his armor easily chinked. Like the ship in the valley, Michael must navigate a very rough course. Exploring his dreams was an adventure worth taking for Michael. He was able to discuss his tumultuous relationship with both parents, who agreed to help him reduce his tension. In some respects, Michael's conflicts reflect those of all teenagers as they try to assert their independence but are not quite ready to separate from their parents. Michael's dream metaphors were unusually graphic in expressing his conflict. He reproduced the dream in art class, a strategy that kept the dream alive for him and further helped him to process the dream content.

MOLLIE

Mollie had just turned 17. Of Indian heritage, from Colombia, South America, Mollie had been adopted when she was five. She has cerebral palsy and walks only with the aid of crutches. Her younger brother, who is also adopted, has Down syndrome. Mollie has a bubbly personality and is somewhat seductive. Her friends tease her about her 30-year-old male friend whom, they say, is sweet on her and whom she "wraps around her finger." He also is physically handicapped. Mollie indicates that she has frequent violent dreams, dreams of falling, dreams of witches. "I worry too much," she reveals. Mollie does not know her background. Even her age is a guess. No records were obtained at her adoption. It is believed that she was abused as a young child. Her nightmares may stem from these early experiences, which are not available to memory in her wakened state.

> I am in my home. Jack and Karl, my brothers, are in their bathtub. Mom and I are in the bathroom. I am sitting on the toilet or on the floor. I am curious. Lizards start coming out of the bathtub—the spigot. Maybe they are chameleons. They are green and "yucky." What are they? I am afraid, squeamish. Mom picks them up with her fingers, wraps them in a towel and throws them downstairs. Mom says, "Is that an old one or maybe you never had it before?"

Mollie was sure it was her bathroom because of the floral wallpaper and the light fixture. Several years ago, when her brothers were three and four years old, Mollie would help her mother by giving them baths. Mollie enjoyed doing this because she felt she was being useful. Now the boys will not let her in the bathroom because they want to be independent. They are six and seven years old, Mollie says, and "I can't stand them." The lizards, she said, had long tails and were scary, fat things. What made them scary, Mollie explained, was the way they moved.

Mollie recalled an incident when she and her friends were at the seashore in Wildwood, New Jersey. They were at the house of a friend. A little boy in the house had a pet chameleon in a cage. He took out the chameleon and came at Mollie to scare her. "I couldn't avoid it," she said. A little later, Mollie and her friends went to the boardwalk. Carla, one of her friends, was pushing Mollie in a wheelchair. They entered a vendor's stall. The proprietor tried to sell Mollie a chameleon. Mollie was again frightened. Carla jokingly threatened to push Mollie into the cage. Mollie was slow to tell her friend she was frightened. The proprietor persisted, following Mollie with the chameleon. "I was going to kill Carla. I was so mad at her. Get me out of here," Mollie said. "Then we went home and had ice cream in the kitchen."

Mollie believes she has been afraid of lizards since she was very young. During a science experiment in school, Mollie was given a worm in a cup. She dropped the cup and accidentally stepped on the worm and killed it. The other students laughed. She remembers having the same feeling she now has toward lizards.

Mollie's mother's question in the dream, "Was that an old one or maybe you never had it before?" related to a recent incident. Mollie and her mother had been cleaning out her closet. Her mother's question related to an old pair of jeans.

Mollie's dream was beginning to make sense to her. She saw the closet cleaning as a dirty job. *Dirty* had another meaning to her. The nudity of her brothers during their bath also had a "dirty" meaning to Mollie. Bathing her brothers made Mollie feel more independent. This dream illustrates that dreams often have more than one meaning.

Glossary

Adrenaline   A hormone, also called epinephrine, that is secreted in times of stress or danger to help prepare the body for "fight or flight."

Alpha waves   Brain waves characteristic of a state of being awake but relaxed.

Amnesia   A partial or total loss of memory of past experiences.

Archetypes   In Jungian psychology, universal themes from myths and legends that influence personality and behavior.

Behaviorism   A branch of psychology that reduces behavior to stimulus-response connections. Behaviorism limits the study of psychology to observable and measurable responses and the conditions associated with those responses.

Brain stem   The central core and most primitive structure of the brain, which begins where the spinal cord enters the skull and is responsible for several critical functions, such as breathing.

Brain waves   Electrical activity produced by different areas of the brain that is measurable using an electroencephalograph (EEG).

Censor   In psychoanalytic theory, the part of the personality that serves as a gatekeeper over which thoughts are allowed entry into conscious awareness.

Cerebral hemisphere   Either of the two interconnected halves of the brain.

Circadian rhythms   Daily cycles of day-night physiological activity and behavior.

Cognitions   Thoughts and ideas that influence behavior and feelings.

Collective unconscious   According to Jungian theory, a group of universal themes in the brain and nervous system that are passed from generation to generation. These themes, called archetypes, appear in myths and legends and symbolically in dreams.

Condensation   The combination of two or more concepts or ideas into a single dream image.

Conscious awareness Private perceptions, images, thoughts, and dreams experienced by an individual.

Cortisol A hormone that prepares the body for stress or emergency, and also prepares an individual to awaken from sleep.

Day residue Dream images that reflect perceptions and events experienced during the preceding day.

Defense mechanisms Processes used by the ego to keep feelings such as guilt and anxiety confined to the unconscious.

Delta waves Brain waves of low frequency and high voltage that are characteristic of Stage 3 sleep.

Dementia Deterioration of intellectual faculties.

Displacement In dream imagery, attribution of motives or characteristics of one person to another.

Dissociation An apparent splitting of conscious awareness or personality during hypnosis or in certain psychological disorders such as amnesia or multiple personalities.

DNA Deoxyribonucleic acid. The basic hereditary material of all organisms, located in the chromosomes.

EEG See **Electroencephalograph**.

Ego The conscious part of the personality that interacts with the external environment and tests reality.

Eidetic imagery The ability to retain visual images with photographic clarity. These images may be recalled in greater detail than is usually possible with memory alone.

Electroencephalograph (EEG) A device used to record the electrical activity of the brain by attaching electrodes to the scalp.

Empirical (noun form is *empiricism*) Referring to the belief that behavior is learned as a result of experience and that knowledge can be gained from objective observation and measurement of behavior.

Experimental psychology The laboratory study of psychological principles governing the behavior of animals and human beings.

Free association   Method used in psychoanalytic therapy in which the patient is instructed to say anything that comes to mind, no matter how trivial or embarrassing it might seem.

Fugue state   A dissociative disorder in which an individual may find him- or herself at a distant place, with no memory of his or her previous life.

Geneticist   Scientist who studies hereditary transmission of physical and personality characteristics.

Gestalt therapy   A form of psychotherapy developed by Fritz Perls on the basis of the idea that people must find their own way in life and accept personal responsibility if they hope to achieve maturity.

Gray matter   A part of the brain that consists of the nerve cell nuclei and appears gray in color.

Hallucinations   Sensory experiences that occur without sensory stimulation and are perceived as real.

Hippocampus   A nerve center in the brain's limbic system that helps process memories for storage.

Hypnosis   An induced, responsive, dream-like state of heightened suggestibility.

Hypothalamus   A part of the limbic system that is instrumental in the storage of memories.

Hysteria   A term used to describe psychological conditions such as blindness, deafness, or paralysis for which there is no known physical cause and a psychological cause is inferred.

Id   The unconscious part of the personality; the seat of the instincts, including aggression and sexual drives.

Identity crisis   A stage in adolescent development in which there is confusion about role; this stage is characterized by experimenting with a variety of behaviors and attitudes, and often involves noncompliance and rebellion.

Insight   A greater depth of awareness and understanding about one's own personality and motivation.

Insomnia A sleep disturbance that involves recurring problems in falling or staying asleep.

Latent content The real, hidden meaning of dreams.

Limbic system A part of the brain related to the control and expression of emotion.

Lucid dreams Dreams in which the dreamer is aware that he or she is dreaming.

Magnetic resonance imaging (MRI) A technique that uses magnetic fields and radio waves to produce computer-generated images to distinguish between different types of soft tissue and structures within the body.

Manifest content The surface content of a dream, taken at face value.

Melatonin A hormone that is secreted by the pineal gland as our eyes register the onset of darkness.

Mentalistic Placing prime significance upon mental events rather than bodily reactions.

Metaphor A visual image in a dream that represents something else to which it is connected through a word association. Metaphors are a specific type of symbol.

Metaphysical Related to speculative or abstract reasoning.

Multiple personality A type of dissociative disorder in which two or more personalities may exist in the same individual. The individual personalities may or may not be aware of each other.

Narcolepsy Sudden, repeated, uncontrollable urges to sleep.

Neocortex The thin, wrinkled surface area of the frontal lobes responsible for integrating, interpreting, and acting on sensory information and memories.

Neologism A new word formed by the combination of two or more words; the new word expresses the meanings of the individual words. A neologism is an example of condensation.

Neurologist A specialist in the diagnosis and treatment of diseases of the nervous system.

Night terrors A sleep disturbance, usually affecting children, in which the person arises from a seemingly deep sleep showing intense fright and being unable to distinguish sleep from reality.

Oscilloscope An electronic instrument that produces a visual display of electron motion on the screen of a cathode ray tube.

Over-determined Having multiple meanings for the same dream image.

Panic An overwhelming, debilitating feeling that something bad is about to happen.

Pineal gland A small structure in the brain. Thought by Descartes to be the site where the soul interacts with the body.

Positron emission tomography (PET) A visual display of brain activity made possible by the injection of radioactive glucose.

Preconscious Thoughts temporarily out of conscious awareness but having the capability to become conscious.

Procedural memory Memory of the processes required to perform tasks that require practice and repetition. Procedural memory may be enhanced by sleep.

Psyche The soul or spirit as distinguished from the body.

Psychoanalysis A theory of neuroses, originated by Sigmund Freud, that assumes a sexual origin of symptoms, an active unconscious, and the use of free association and dream analysis in treatment.

Psychoanalytic thought Thinking on the basis of psychoanalysis that influences literature, art, philosophy, and popular conceptions of the nature of man.

Psychoses (singular is *psychosis*) Severe mental disorders in which thinking and emotion are so impaired as to undermine contact with reality.

REM sleep A sleep period characterized by rapid eye movements and irregular breathing.

Repression The defense mechanism used to keep unconscious motives submerged and prevent anxiety.

Resistance Efforts of the personality to prevent frightening, unacceptable impulses from entering conscious awareness.

Reticular activating system A system of nerve paths and connections within the brain stem that is associated with arousal mechanisms.

Sleep apnea A cessation of breathing during sleep.

Sleep spindles Bursts of rapid, rhythmic brain wave activity during Stage 2 sleep as measured on an EEG.

Stimuli (singular is *stimulus*) A specific physical energy that impinges on a receptor sensitive to that kind of energy. Any situation or event that is the occasion of an organism's response.

String theory A new approach to understanding how the universe is organized that is based on the notion that the smallest units of matter are minute strings of energy.

Subjective events Events within the conscious awareness of the individual but not directly observable.

Sudden infant death syndrome (SIDS) The unexplained death of infants in their cribs. The incidence of SIDS has been greatly reduced by instructing parents to place infants in bed on their backs.

Superego A component of personality that has split off from the ego and represents the conscience of the individual.

Symbol A dream image that stands for something else.

Trait An enduring predisposition to think, feel, and behave in certain ways.

Trait theory The theory that human personality may be characterized by scores that an individual obtains on a series of scales, each of which represents a trait or dimension of his or her personality.

Transcend To pass beyond a human limit.

Unconscious Thoughts that are more permanently beyond conscious awareness than preconscious thought.

Vision quest   Native American ritual that facilitates personal growth through dreams. A coming-of-age journey taken by Native American teenagers to explore their dreams, acquire knowledge and self-understanding, and add to their cultural heritage.

Visual cortex   The center for vision located at the rear of the brain.

Bibliography

Aserinsky, E., and N. Kleitman. "Regularly Occurring Periods of Eye Mobility and Concomitant Phenomena During Sleep." *Science* 118(1953): 273–274.

Brink, S. M., J.A.B. Allan, and W. Boldt. "Symbolic Representation of Psychological States in the Dreams of Women With Eating Disorders." *Canadian Journal of Counseling* 29(1995): 332–344.

Bruce, R. *Astral Dynamics: A New Approach to Out-of-Body Experiences.* Charlottesville, VA: Hampton Roads Publishing Company, 1999.

Carroll, L. A. *Alice's Adventures in Wonderland* and *Through the Looking Glass.* New York: Alfred A. Knopf, 1992.

Dement, W. C., and C. Vaughan. *The Promise of Sleep.* New York: Dell, 2000.

Foulkes, D. *Dreaming: Cognitive Psychological Analysis.* Hillsdale, NJ: Lawrence Erlbaum, 1985.

Freud, S. *The Interpretation of Dreams.* New York: The Modern Library, 1950.

Galley, J.M.C. *Dream Motifs: A Comparison of Dream Content for Depressed and Nondepressed Adolescents.* Doctoral dissertation, Department of Psychology, Pace University, New York. Pace University Library, 1994.

Gillin, J. C., S.P.A. Drummand, J. L. Stricker, E. C. Wong, and R. B. Buxton. "Brain Activity Is Visibly Altered Following Sleep Deprivation." *Nature* (2000).

Gorman, C. "Why We Sleep." *Time* (December 20, 2004): 46–59.

Hall, C. S. *The Meaning of Dreams.* New York: McGraw-Hill. 1966.

Hall, C., and R. Van de Castle. *The Content Analysis of Dreams.* New York: Appleton Press, 1966.

Hartman, E. "The Strangest Sleep Disorder." *Psychology Today* 15(1981): 14–18.

Irwin, L. "Walking in the Sky: Visionary Traditions of the Great Plains." *Great Plains Quarterly* 14(1994): 257–271.

Kripke, D. F., and R. N. Simons. "Average Sleep, Insomnia, and Sleeping-pill Use." *Sleep Research* 5(1976): 110.

Kutas, M. "Vent-related Brain Potential (ERP) Studies of Cognition During Sleep: Is It More Than a Dream?" *Sleep and Cognition*, eds. R. R. Bootzin, J. F. Kihlstrom, and D. Schacter. Washington, D.C.: American Psychological Association, 1990, p. 223.

La Berge, S. D. "Lucid Dreams: Directing the Act as It Happens." *Psychology Today* 15(1981): 48–57.

Maltzberger, J. T. "Dreams and Suicide." *Suicide and Life-threatening Behavior* 23(1993): 55–62.

McGrath, M. J., and D. G. Cohen. "REM Sleep Facilitation of Adaptive Waking Behavior: A Review of the Literature." *Psychological Bulletin* 85(1978): 24–57.

McKeller, P. *Imagination and Thinking*. New York: Basic Books, 1957.

Monroe, R. *Journeys Out of the Body*. Garden City, N.Y.: Doubleday, 1971.

Palumbo, S. *Dreaming and Memory: A New Information-processing Model*. New York: Basic Books, 1978.

Perls, F. S. *Ego, Hunger, and Aggression: The Beginning of Gestalt Therapy*. New York: Random House, 1969.

Porte, H. "The Sleeping Brain." *Arts & Sciences Newsletter* Winter 2004. Cornell University: 2–3.

Restak, R. *Brainscapes*. New York: Hyperion, 1995.

Rycroft, C. *The Innocence of Dreams*. New York: Pantheon, 1979.

Sayers, J. *Boy Crazy: Remembering Adolescence, Therapies and Dreams*. New York: Rutledge, 1998.

Seligman, M.E.P. *Learned Optimism: How To Change Your Mind and Your Life*. New York: A. A. Knopf, 1990.

Seligman, M.E.P., and A. Yellen. "What Is a Dream?" *Behavior Research & Therapy* 25(1987): 1–24.

Watson, J. B., and R. Raynor. "Conditioned Emotional Reactions." *Journal of Experimental Psychology* 3(1920): 1–14.

Winegar, R. K., and R. Levin. "Sex Differences in the Dreams of Adolescents." *Sex Roles* 36(1997): 503–516.

Winson, J. "The Meaning of Dreams." *Scientific American* 263(1996): 86–96.

Further Reading

Atkinson, R., R. C. Atkinson, and E. R. Hilgard. *Introduction to Psychology*, 4th ed. New York: Harcourt Brace, 1983.

Blos, P. *The Adolescent Passage: Developmental Issues.* New York: International Universities Press, 1979.

Calafano, S. *Children's Dreams in Clinical Practice.* New York: Plenum, 1990.

Clark, A. C. *2001: A Space Odyssey.* New York: New American Library, 1968.

Cook, C. A., R. D. Caplan, and H. Wolowitz. "Nonwaking Responses to Waking Stressors: Dreams and Nightmares." *Journal of Applied Social Psychology* 3(1990): 199–206.

Corey, G. *Theory and Practice of Counseling and Psychotherapy*, 3rd ed. Pacific Grove, CA: Brooks/Cole, 1986.

Ehrenwald, J. *From Medicine Man to Freud.* New York: Dell, 1956.

Erikson, E. H. *Childhood and Society.* New York: Norton, 1963.

Esman, A. H. "The Dream Screen in an Adolescent." *Psychoanalytic Quarterly* 31(1962): 250–251.

Fancher, R. E. *Pioneers of Psychology*, 2nd ed. New York: W. W. Norton, 1990.

Feist, J. *Theories of Personality*, 2nd ed. Chicago: Holt, Rinehart & Winston, 1990.

Frazer, J. G. *The Illustrated Golden Bough: A Study in Magic and Religion.* New York: Macmillan, 1922.

Freud, S. *Psychopathology of Everyday Life.* New York: Mentor Books, 1951.

Galton, F. "The Visions of Sane Persons." *Proceedings of the Royal Institute of Great Britain* 9(1882): 644–655.

Glenn, J., and I. Bernstein. "The Fantasy World of the Child as Revealed in Art, Play, and Dreams." *The Neurotic Child and Adolescent*, ed. M. H. Etezady. Northvale, NJ: Jason Aronson, 1990, pp. 319–347.

Mooncroft, W. *Sleep, Dreaming, and Sleep Disorders*, 2nd ed. Lanham, MD: University Press of America, 1993.

Myers, D. G. *Psychology*, 4th ed. New York: Worth, 1995.

Schredl, M. "Creativity and Dream Recall." *Journal of Creative Behavior* 29(1995): 16–24.

Tolkien, J.R.R. *Lord of the Rings*. New York: Harper Collins, 2002.

Webb, W. B. *Sleep: The Gentle Tyrant*, 2nd ed. Bolton, MA: Anker Publishing, 1992.

Websites

Dream catchers
http://www.nativetech.org/dreamcat/dreminst.html

REM sleep
http://www.sfn.org/content/Publications/BrainBriefings/rem_sleep.html

Sleep deprivation
http://health.ucsd.edu/news/2000_02_09_Sleep.html

■ Index

About the Author

Marvin Rosen is a doctorate-level, licensed, clinical and school psychologist. He has worked in a variety of mental health and school settings, providing clinical services for children and adults, and has conducted a private practice of psychology. Dr. Rosen has authored seven college- or graduate-level textbooks dealing with the habilitation of mentally handicapped persons. He has also written several books for high school students, dealing with stress, anxiety, trauma, dreams, and love. He has served as a consulting editor for Chelsea House Publishers.

Dr. Rosen lives with his wife in Media, Pennsylvania. He has four grown children and six grandchildren (and still counting). Besides writing, he enjoys hiking, swimming, and gardening.

Picture Credits